Charlies Guide

13 13
PRESS

Charlies Guide

Roy Thomas Dow

Copyright © 2019 Roy Thomas Dow
Charlies Guide Originally published Balboa Press.

This fully revised second edition;
Copyright May 2021 Roy Thomas Dow.

All rights reserved. No part of this book may be used or reproduced by any means, graphic, electronic or mechanical, including photocopying, recording, taping or by any information storage retrieval system without the written permission of the author except in the case of brief quotations embodied in critical articles and reviews.

1331 press
PO Box 228
Wondai. Qld. 4606 Australia
Details may be found on roydow.com

With Gratitude.
To all in awareness – It is an honour to serve all, with a view towards growth.
Thank you for being here

Note to the Reader.
My intention with this book is to share awareness, and sow seeds of light and love.
If either is achieved, I am truly humbled by duty and honour realised.

General Disclaimer.
I offer information of a general nature to help you in your quest for emotional and spiritual well-being. I express my own opinions as I am entitled to do. Any interpretations of these opinions are simply more opinions.
In the event you use any of the information in this book for yourself, which is your right based on freewill of the individual, the author and publisher assume no responsibility for your actions whatsoever.

ISBN: 978-1-922499-07-3 (Print Book)
ISBN: 978-1-922499-08-0 (E-Book)
ISBN: TBC   (Audible Book)
1331 press – Rev. Date: 2206-2022.
Cover and layout design – in-house.

To Charlie,
and all the children of the world,
(big & small).

Remember,
the greatest love, is born within,
and expressed, unconditionally
without.

~*~

Other titles in the 'charlies' series

charlies guide

charlies poem

charleis plan

charlies way

All titles published <u>exclusively,</u>

by 1331PRESS

PRESS

Contents

~*~

Preface	3
Inspired by a Stone (a poem)	5
Yesterday	9
Today	65
Tomorrow	119
Imagine, ME (a poem)	139
Conclusion	143
Limitation	155
Peace not War (a poem)	163
Don't Panic! Take Care Beans (Not a warning, just truth)	165
Change begins now!	173
All aboard! (a poem)	180
My daily (anytime) prayer	182

Preface

~*~

"What will you do?"

...

"I will leave a guide."

...

"To what end?"

...

"To encourage assessment, and future growth;
to talk of things that answer questions;
to demonstrate the great simplicity of it all;
that they may walk in the present, and create
using the divine awareness as their only compass,
free - to follow their heart."

.
...
......
....

abracadabra

That awareness, is, everything; is enough

Enough to start and go on with.

For an eternity.

Consider this to begin a journey unlike any other. For here in these pages, even as you read now, the truth of your limitless ability is only very slowly beginning to awaken within. But awaken it is!
To simply think of everything as *knowing expressed*. Even energy. Which is created by knowing, so that we become aware of the energy it just produced.

Consider how awareness (knwowing) and nothing else, is all there is.
You could close your eyes right now and just spend some time, thinking about how everything is just awareness.
So, I am, and that you are, and furthermore, *all is*, is just a simple truth.
With nothing more than this information as a foundation in *your awareness*, read on and discover all you need take you onto your next step in your own personal evolution.
As we consider the awareness of another entity of course, that many call god. Who I prefer to call, the big g.

~*~

*"Remember, the WORD we hear,
is enough to change our BEing."*

Roy Thomas Dow. 20122021

~*~

Inspired by a Stone

(a poem)

A young man twenty-two years full,
looked high into the sky
and saw the beauty of a bird
and wished that he could fly.

The bird flew down towards him
and did land upon his hand
the young man smiled inwardly
for all had gone as planned.

The young man asked his secret
that of flying would he tell
said the bird, it's just inherited
d'you know I sing as well?

The young man laughed, I'm teasing you
for I too can fly high
is this more tricks, the bird replied
or just perhaps a lie?

Man cannot fly without machine
no strength, can't stand the pace
I can and do, the young man said
with style and with grace.

Some would say I dream too much
it's all within my mind
for you it's purely functional
your body's so inclined.

The hen just pecks the ground to feed
and never tries to fly
tis sad her talent goes to waste
no fun before she'll die.

You've a talent, use it, test it
fly high all around
fulfil your wishes hopes and dreams
before you're underground.

Try to see it as it is,
a freedom that we share
and join the ranks of those
who live their lives without a care.

A voice inside says let your heart
and mind and dreams fly high
then always you'll find love and joy
your youth will never die.

You've strange ideas and dreams
the bird said, yet I feel they're good
I know we can do anything
if we tell ourselves we could.

I know this, said the young man
yet we only do a third
of what we could do if we wanted.
such is life replied the bird.

Both laughed and smiled, both got up
each went their separate ways
the bird vowed to the young man
I shall fly for all my days.

Now, reader look inside your soul
I know it sounds absurd
but which one are you, grounded hen
I doubt the flying bird?

So, if you are the grounded hen
the time has come to fly
shed the cloak of doldrums
spread your wings and search the sky.

Roy Thomas Dow. 29th September 1982

Yesterday

Yesterday has gone.

…

With but a single, simple, expression of love, all that is, is;

one spark of an idea;

one dream to explore;

to see and create.

.
…
……
………

abracadabra

("I create what I speak")
…
See
"as I believe, so shall it be!"
…

"It is NEVER a question of,
that which you desire, I deliver unto thee, No.
It is simply a case of, such as YOU DESIRE,
YOU, deliver unto SELF"
(the big g, me, I, you)

What is 'faith'?
Is it something like love?
Something else we cannot see?
Something intangible, perhaps?
Yet, something we can grow.
Equally, as with,
Belief & Trust,
Hope & Desire,
Faith?
I have complete faith in the big g.
Who is the big g?
That would be our creator.
An entity for which I cannot offer a single description, in the sense of form, for there is no form, separate from all that is.
That is, as far as my awareness is concerned.
The Love of my creator is found in all things in awareness.
In the Universe. The Single Song.
The nature of my creator is infinite.

I, as an expression of the creator, ergo myself, am here extending the experience in the expansion of awareness of other self. The other self, being me and you. I utilise my freewill to create all in my awareness according to my most heartfelt desires.
My journey here is the only expression of self I know, with a goal of growth of self.
I base this on the premise that if there is only self, there can only BE more of self. To this end, I have created awareness, which is infinite; infinitely intelligent energy, filling an infinite space, in my own infinite awareness.
And so, when you are the beginning and the end, the alpha and the omega, when you have been and seen and done it all, the only thing left is to do, is to extend yourself.
Here we are in an experiment if you will, as individual entities

with freewill and a blindfold over the existence of all there is to know in awareness.

This is the Veil of Confusion.

Because of this, instead of saying we only use 10% of our brain capacity, why not consider, that we only see, say, less than 10% of creation in our awareness due to our limited sight brought about by the Veil of Confusion.

In this way, there is no bias from expectation, through knowing. "I know the big g is there, so we can just enjoy all, fearlessly."

By comparison, the development of FEAR through a sense of uncertainty over so much (a result of the Veil of Confusion), produces notions in creation that are not possible when all is known in awareness (to whatever level of awareness you are currently experiencing).

In this way, I, we, or collectively I, create a world blind to the truth of its surroundings, of its connection to all that is, which after all is simply the LOVE of ONE.

Love is the focussed awareness of infinite intelligence, the fabric of the universe in infinite potential.

I believe. I love. I have a desire for a union with the ONE.

This union will complete my awareness.

A wholeness.

A contentment.

Bliss.

Success in this endeavour comes through the growth in awareness, through self-control and focus on a task.

With this growth, comes the awareness of self from the perspective of soul. The expression of the creator as the you, you know in your awareness, as you the Individual. The Human Animal, the tamed beast; eventually (hopefully), guided by the divine spirit. And so, Divine Human walks the earth.

We could consider an image, as just too 2 D?

Perhaps the UNIverse, is just too 3 D?

The big g appears to BE, beyond the fabric of what we call space, beyond what we think of as the Universe, BEing the creator of the universe itself!

Remembering that we are created in the same image as the creator, suggests then, that we too are beyond what we perceive as space/time (or even Time/Space). We too, are outside looking in.

All that we *sense* currently, is outside of what we know is the inside of the true side. Only the big g is outside. Of whom we are created, the same.

An analogy here may serve to help you see who's what and where.

Life here and the computer game analogy.

Many people around the world are aware of computer games and how we can remotely control a character on screen.

So, imagine a world where you create a character. The character is you and exists in this world we call Planet Earth.

You control this character to some degree, whereby you can intervene directly to affect the awareness of your character, by dropping hints about what you want your character to do and BEcome aware of.

The character (you), is in this world to learn. You do this by surviving in this world, and choosing the best course of thought, speech and action according to your awareness of what is and is not desirable. You can join in with the world or do something different.

There is no limit to what the character (you), can or cannot do, although all action has reactions.

These changes can sometimes be favourable and sometimes less so.

Events are cyclic in nature. This ensures that if you miss the learning experience offered by circumstance, it will naturally build to a point of potential in awareness again. All cycles repeat as needed.

The original object of the exercise was to develop an environment where what was called life grew, evolved and survived. To guide the growth of the human BEan in awareness, evolving into a BEing of Cooperation, Harmony and Love. This is achieved through realisations (for example), in the work efficiency, in the survival of many over one.

Where there is greater energy, there is greater force for change!

So, the mindset of many can influence the whole for the greater good of the whole.

Now there's a thought…

Please note here!

Success is based on the ability of the individual to control the notions of self from the perspective of the human BEast, and evolve towards an expanding awareness of love, selflessness and service to others as a means of rapid growth of self. This text offers much to 'see', and so embrace into your reality as awareness. Thereby expanding your awareness.

Having built good foundations for strong growth, the speed of progress towards an awareness of the divine self is limited only by your own imagination. One could consider this and change your focus.

Back to the game analogy.

We see the character in the game is oblivious to the presence of the player.

This is the same as the Veil of Confusion here.

This lack of awareness about our true nature, our origins, and our potential, allow for the creation of an extension of the awareness of the creator, so that we seem like an independent BEing, existing within our own sense of awareness. It's like a pocket within the whole, with curtains to limit the view out. But always remember, we are created as an extension of the awareness of the creator to provide growth in the awareness of other self, and that self is the big g.

If you do not explore here and find that inner you, and accept your responsibility towards the notion of self and the task of self-control, honesty with self, love of self, then you may return to the beginning of the same density elsewhere. Effectively reduced to/ returned to dust, in a figurative sense here. This is no sacrifice as this is big g acting on self, remember that always.

You may simply suffer the fates of all tortured by your presence here before death. To allow you to find awareness and balance in the experiences.

Reading here, one can begin to embrace the notion of a separateness. One could consider the existence of a self, outside of this limited awareness!

One could picture the earth from space, off in the distance, and maybe see a field of energy enveloping the whole planet and much of its surrounding space.

The simpler truth of course, would be the understanding of the limitations built into our sensory systems.

Limited awareness.

Yet there are no limitations in the nature of self. Neither are there limitations on the expression of self. Much, simply exists to be overcome in some way.

This understanding is offered in shared awareness to assist in the expansion of self.

To understand is to see in awareness and convey for the benefit of other self, growth in awareness.

The lack of awareness we experience here is relatively unique in the universe. It was created to accelerate the process of polarisation towards love, which we polarise ourselves towards in our awareness, through the use of love as a creative medium.

We mostly always retain the notion of limited sight here.

Aware that struggle and difficulty serve as catalyst for change.

That introspection serves to bring self-awareness.
That through self-awareness we can see cycles.
That we can see opportunities for change through breaking cycles and growing. Cycles that may have been evident in family lines for generations!
The lack of clear sight suggests to us we are alone and need to survive. This is how we have an awareness of freewill. How we seem to create in our own right, which of course we do and do not. Yet with a growing awareness of truth, the choice of path may BEcome clearer. We may begin to sense a need for greater self-control, self-responsibility and a need to discover the process of self-resurrection!
Sowing seeds in yourself with a sense of expectation, of joy of... Love.
As you believe (BE live/within), so shall it be!
Experience it, to create it. Feel it through your senses to create your reality.
Rushing on comes the emotion to build the strongest foundations, the emotions cementing in the experience.
Is this hinting at the nature of the big g and perhaps an insight into the origin of the UNIverse? Of course! Everything does if you look at it.
Let us consider that we can truly become at one with our creator, which one could say is the end game. We can see we need to grow some first, as we need to raise our own level of vibration.
And so, it goes on. Until we BEcome at ONE with source in the eighth octave. At which point we lose all sense of self as we merge with the creator. This is *not* possible without a matching awareness and vibe'.
I ask myself, how can we best serve in the growth of the awareness of all in potential? Here, I share my awareness to assist, as it can.
What do we need to know now to sufficiently expand our

awareness whereby we have the potential for self-control and the freedom to express ourselves without encroaching on the experience of another?

This includes reducing all our negative mental, verbal and physical projections upon all other self regardless of perceived identity.

Self-control is a challenge. Tame the BEast, the Human Animal.

The human animal that destroys. That kills.

That the human animal is weak and easily led because it has little or no awareness of truth, is easily observed here in this awareness. Among so many; perhaps one could say the majority?

On a personal level, I find it impossible to conceive of an awareness, whereby the life experienced here by other self is taken. Yet we are all mostly aware of instances of such tragically low vibration demonstrated in awareness.

Awareness IS a process of elevation.

The intertwined relationships of so much energy in chaos is alarming in a way.

It's almost as if the big g is out of control? But then we pause and consider the nature of the big g.

Which brings me to the 4 fundamental questions that all human animals may need to be aware of.

I believe that BEcoming aware of the potential for growth in the individual's own awareness (as in ours), to the point where we begin to acquire control over the human beast (our Base instincts – e.g. Fear Anger/Fight or Flight), through the acquisition of truth into our own awareness which is experienced as reality, in the process of expanding mind.

Then, the balance of awareness shifts within what we perceive as the individual, towards awareness of (and potential descending of, in a figurative sense), the Divine Awareness to create the Divine Human.

To walk on this earth, but not BE of this earth.

As of this moment during the final editing, I am intending to share my awareness in the steps for engaging with the notion of a process of personal resurrection.

But enough of this. Let's get back to the 4 fundamental questions that I believe need answering.
1. Who what when where why - the big g?
2.   Who what when where why - the universe/creation?
3.   Who what when where why - us?
4.   Who what when where why - next?

We have begun to explore truth in the preceding pages, let's continue on.

Current human endeavours are focussed on what we can see. As we can see little truth, is it any wonder that we feel perplexed at times?

We can look back, of course we can.

We can guess about this or that.

We can test and prove that there is, a confidence, based on this or that outcome...

That in all probability, we believe, based on our best estimates, including the assessment of the most up to date data ... well, we still don't truly know; until of course, we do.

We don't have the definitive evidence... or do we?

And until we have access to all the information (which is infinite), we will never really know... or will we?

When we are one with the creator of course.

Again, we can pause here and consider that we know that everything in view, is subject to position in reference to us a viewer. This is true as we look out.

We assess and try to understand based on here, when we should explore within more, to know more about the inner self, to help in the outer perception!

To picture all. From the start to the finish and back again… to simply see and BE in awe, filled with wonder at the majesty and great simplicity of it all.

And then there is to not know, to not BE aware. Truly, there, but for the grace of god go I.

To nurture the desire within to seek.

To see the most infinitesimally small detail in all its wonder and glory.

In the beginning…   (which beginning?).

To fuel the whole of creation, with one single principle.

With that single, simple principle being repeated over and over in an infinite dance of cause & effect; Resulting in constant change, through action. Infinite potential exists always.

But what is the meaning of life?

The meaning of life is that creation took place and that the big g exists.

BUT HOW?

[

As of 07102021, I have posted a video on youtube, sharing my awareness of the big g, creation and us, plus the notion of 'god particle' and the creation of the principle of consciousness. A link is below.

Type this into your search engine.

https://youtu.be/bKoECdfq1GA

]

The purpose of life is to BE. BUT WHY?

To grow, through BEing.

To BE, we do, to the extent that we are, which is dependent on what we think, which reflects our awareness.

It is your own awareness that ultimately seals your "future" regarding how you will or will not progress, subject to your vibratory rate.

In this way, we see the simple logic of the process of progress. Dependant solely on our own disposition.

Devoid of intervention from the creator or anyone else; save the nudges of catalysts to encourage choice, one way or the other.

HOWEVER, consider this…

When you have a 'tank' full of potential that has 'stewed' for a while, at the end of the process do you discard that which grows in different ways? Or do you 'Contain' it, to allow for the constant development of that nature (not of the Path).

This would BE a place of the lowest vibration! That of the savage BEast? Perhaps called the hells?

The question still follows.

Would YOU, ONLY contain low vibratory energy during the long process or allow it to constantly build-up, to balance creation, as in the balance of good and evil? NO.

Why? Because it moves away from the original concept of growth of self, through the notion of other self, adding to that which *is* Self.

How can the awareness of Beast, blend in harmony with the big g?

ALL so bold, yet this truly is just the beginning of your journey! Understanding/awareness comes with progression.

And so, you start the whole process again because it works. The notion of mass 'death' is not realised, as death does not exist in the nature of the big g, merely repurposing. Besides, is it not all just "Self" affected – True

So, will the big g repurpose your "Immortal Awareness" to begin the same journey again?

Choice at every turn. That would be YOURS!

There is NO future per se, neither past.

ALL is present;

WHY - HOW?

Because everything is realised in the present.

SEE. WE are not part of this process, BUT – ALIGNED with it, so to speak.

We can all embrace change. Change is brought about by action.
Action is the result of desire.
Desire is fuelled by awareness.
The infinite cycle of change is the core principle of creation.
While awareness is infinite, awareness in individuals is variable, in this current experience and beyond.
We see evidence of this in the behaviour of all of us.
Awareness is what we consider thought.

Everything is awareness!

"abracadabra'"("I create what I speak"). We speak in our awareness, which is what we label the mind.
"I create what I speak", suggests that what we say, we create, magically somewhere. Which, in a way is true.
The magic is of course love. The fuel of creation in the literal sense.
Let us consider the big g then.
The big g IS the ONE and only creator of all that is in awareness, regardless of where that awareness is or how it's perceived to BE.
So, who then, who is God?
God is the creator.
Call the creator by any name and the entity remains the same.
The purpose of all remains the same.
Though through the errors associated with many religions, through the corruptions of self, the nature of god and god's relationship to the human BEan has BEcome tainted with the notions of the HUMAN Animal, that IS the BEast.
The notion of control. Of punishment. Of right and wrong. Of rules and regulations, doctrines and guidelines to suit the men who spew forth their lies, based on nonsense!
That the creator, would wish to kill any form of life is a nonsense... or is it?

That what we think of as life and death is a part of this awareness of limited creation, and it serves as a reality for experiential purposes only as we attempt to control the BEast and learn about love and creation.
"What's god got to do, got to do with it…"
Again, back to god, only this time, let's go 2,3 and 4 also.
Who what when where and why god, the universe, us, next?

god - *the big g*
who - *creator*.
What - (I am that I am) - *infinite knowing & awareness*.
When - *Now. There is only now*. Past is now. Future is now.
SEE – NOW!
Where - everywhere as perceived
Why - Good Question.
Well, it is the nature of the big g to infinitely express self.
As the big g, I have created everything. I AM everything, and everything is in my awareness.
ALERT!!!   "…everything is in my awareness."
The final creative challenge left unrealised in my own awareness, the only real creative challenge left, was to create myself as other self (awareness) in my awareness.
This, is the creation of the universe and all in it.
So, the big g is *outside of the universe*.
We, us, we are *outside of the universe*.
Both as awareness; albeit ours is currently severely limited due to our limited experience.
And when we pass, note we are still outside of the universe, but no longer tied by 5 senses and limited sight. We see fully, according to our level of awareness.
Always growing, until we reach ONENESS with the big g.
Which we can obviously only do when we reach the matching level of vibration.
How else can we harmonise?

So, the Universe…
It was created with the word or breath of god, records say. And this is true.
Consider all things. Picture the electromagnetic scale.
It begins at a finite point. This was the first sound?
I see this as a single pulse if you will. With the lowest possible frequency and energy. With that initial pulse, the first wave rolled, and continues.
Everything repeats in nature and we can see how this is so. When we close our eyes, as we sit in pitch black, in our awareness, we see a single pulse of light. A spark.
In the empty black nothing of our awareness we create light. See it in your forehead area. It may tickle.
We could not measure the black nothingness, yet with a single pulse of light we have created infinite black. It cannot be measured. Yet, by virtue of the presence of light, all blackness exists as potential light.
Through the focussing of awareness, attention on the point of light, we recreate the pulse, again and again until its repetition is such that it is constant and continuous, never ending.
God focusses attention of the one point and we get fixed bright light, glowing. Increasing in intensity as it soars up the electromagnetic scale.
The frequency and the energy levels increase without stopping.
It becomes infinite light, with infinite energy.
Now understand here, that as all things can be referenced on the scale, this means that once infinite energy was achieved, the process of beginning and going to infinity suggests all possible building blocks of creation have been made. All potential frequencies experienced.
The only action left to do was to construct every possible thing in every possible way, to create anything and everything according to desire, need or purpose.

All with infinite intelligence. The same infinite intelligence we have access to. That we can use as directed by our own divine compass.

The very compass that will guide you back to the creator to BEcome at ONE with source as it were.

So, that's god and the universe, what about US?

Well, as I've said, we are extensions of the awareness of god. Here to learn of the power of creation which is love. That's the purpose in this awareness.

There are billions upon billions of individual awareness's growing in the universe.

Another truth to BE aware of is that awareness is found in all things.

This nature is an intelligence. A divine intelligence. It is the essence of our own nature.

An awareness of everything, infinite awareness.

Also, BE aware that the first intelligence here that converted sunlight to energy, is still present and active in every cell in the perceived creation. This of course includes our own shell, the human animal body.

We constantly interact with this connected intelligence, whether that is by choice or not.

Our emotive responses impacts the shell!

We can of course, interact with the intelligence. Our desires are creative forces invoking love based on our intensity of desire, our passion, our yearning.

Like the ultimate desires for an awareness of all things.

A true Awakening!

Full awareness. As in the resurrection of self. Demonstrating self-control, self-responsibility and love of self.

More on this later.

Never accept fear, simply question the reasoning as well as the prsenting circumstances. Engage with intelligence and awareness of presence, and so truth.

It must be a nudge from the big g so we can BE accepting and show gratitude for the sacrifice of other intelligence, that serves you/us to honour its duty as perceived by the notion of self.

Then think about stuff and try to grow! Take decisive action to make things better for you as well as others.

Here, and in all things, one can seek balance.

ALL negative behaviour is influenced by the BEAST.

It displays an animal of low vibration.

It shows an individual who is NOT in control.

They are potentially dangerous, one might consider. Draining you of vital energies! Threatening your very opportunities for growth in awareness here; yet one could always argue that interaction with them is part of your story?

I must of course point out that were someone aware to this extent, I feel that a natural tendency to move away from that energy/person/human animal would be apparent in the awareness.

This could be based on several things. Maybe the sense of self-preservation (the preservation of species through fight or flight), is in play here.

Or perhaps some growth in your awareness that allows you to see the truth before you. And so, you understand that what you experience as behaviour in another, is in fact error and not conducive to growth. That the behaviour is of the nature of the BEAST that is the human animal, not so much the divine you.

Here we can pause and become more aware of the two processes. We can grow moment by moment, expanding our awareness as our unconditional love develops for self and other self. This is a slower opening of the flower, one might say. Slow and steady, step by step, inch by inch.

The more we strive to grow in our understanding of Love, the more we will influence others in positive loving ways and

reinforce the love we feel within ourselves, so to speak.
This path to love IS the ONLY path.
ANY and ALL other PATHS, simply demonstrate you are lost!
Know this.
Anyone that seeks to control you or punish you mentally, verbally or physically, is not in control of themselves from a spiritual perspective.

The BEAST appears to BE in control. Look around the globe and witness the atrocities of men and women. Even children killing others because an adult told them to.

What can you say of the minds and the awareness of these adults that effectively murder the suicide bomber children? Complicit in every way.

Yes, you could say these are the actions of god, because god creates all things. Yet a true examination of context, here, in an awareness where the knowing, is unapparent, the actions are seemingly, of an unaware awareness with regard the one true creator, and as such, these actions are singularly the action of a BEast awareness. The ego of the human animal, and not the actions of a human mind aware of the truth of the ONE true creator. They are not the actions of someone in control of self spiritually.

So, they are expressions of an awareness that is seemingly at odds with the intentions of our creator for growth towards the big g.

Not the actions of someone displaying unconditional love for all, NO.

Perhaps more importantly, they are not the actions of an individual, that is ACTIVE on the ONE path.

Again, there but for the grace of god go I.

People in power everywhere are only interested in the compliance of others to inflate their own sense of self-importance.
Egos run amok.
Pack control dominates. Children are everywhere!

Recognise them and distance yourself from them. Stay on your personal spiritual path.

No sacrifice is too great to engage with the pursuit of divine awareness.

If you cannot deal with a BEan that is or appears to BE unbalanced, arm yourself with acceptance and love.

Tolerance is born of knowing.

Learn and grow in the difficulty, then rise like a phoenix from the ashes, born of the fires that fuel the very change itself.

Here see the foundations of wisdom BEing laid!

The vast majority of all Religious books contain details of our body and how we resurrect ourselves.

This information, and in-fact all perceived esoteric, information, could be revealed to all without hesitation or judgement of any kind.

The fact that it CAME means it must BE DELIVERED en masse.

That any, TINY hooman bean could successfully determine what should be revealed to the masses in awareness and what shouldn't, is such a tragic error on the part of the ego-soaked beans that perpetuate this farce!

Why was the stuff written in the first place? Silly, Silly Beans everywhere! The egos of little people have a lot to answer for. But such is the Nature of the Beast. Such is the nature of the big g perhaps? To cause frustration as a catalyst for change? Or simply the over-inflated egos of little human Beans, grasping at anything and everything to justify their existence, and make them feel better about themselves. Feeling that they are superior to any and all that does not share their sense of knowing and privilege.

In reality, the truth always comes as you ask for it. Bit by bit.

So, what's Next?

Well, you may BE so gross, you only seek sleep on passing! You exist as a simple animal perhaps?

Or, you awake again, somewhere in time/space, with or without awareness of all, to redo, whatever you need to experience truth.
Consider this. How an awareness of truth is a kill or cure perhaps?
If you do not force yourself to develop, you wil not develop!
You may wake up and realise this is now the 4th density awareness.

~*~

To focus on the progression of change is to see and be a part of that which you observe.
Think about that a while!

~*~

To see the cause and effect. To cherish and love. To desire with passion.
The intricate subtleties of the microscopic Mitochondria, the first life to utilise the emitted rays of the sun. The divine life principle that exists in ALL, derives energy from light/love. When we create, we use love/light.
If each one of our cells has the potential to utilise the sun's energy, can we communicate with our collective cells to begin to use that energy and reduce the amount of low vibration food we use to sustain our human vehicle? I would say yes.
In fact, due to our own divine nature and creative potential, could we not exist as divine spirit walking this earth, fuelled by nothing more than Light/Love?
Again, the answer in my awareness, is yes.
The mysteries we perceive in nature are part of our own design inasmuch as we utilise this shell vehicle to increase our exposure to experience, and thus expand, our awareness,

which is the .
This natural design. All brought about through cause and effect.
Labels are stepping stones of understanding. A common ground to discuss and share here in this arena of limited sight. But what is god's design then?
God's design is one of simplicity.

All is derived from, and can BE returned to, that from which it came.

This displays as we play with numbers. 3, 6 and 9 are interesting numbers.
Mentioned as intrinsic to understanding the universe, along with vibration, frequency and energy, according to Mr Nikola Tesla. I agree. See below.
[
Please Note.
I will have shared a video showing a graphic representation of creation for easier assimilation into awareness.
I also refer to frequency, energy and vibration, along with the significance of 3 6 9. It includes the GOD particle and the principle of consciousness.
A link to the video, which is one of several (some short, some long), is here.
https://youtu.be/bKoECdfq1GA
"Roy Dow" on Youtube
]
Here we might as well discuss exactly how god created space.
IN THE BEGINNING, WAS THE WORD, AND THE WORD WAS GOD…

This is the story of creation. It went something like this.

In the beginning – Creation +
By Roy Thomas   23082021

In the beginning, there was nothing.

In the mind's eye of the creator, just as we do in our own, the creator created light.

This was done through the focus of the awareness of the creator upon a single point. From zero vibration, frequency and energy, to infinite vibration, frequency and energy. *Experiencing all possible vibrations at the beginning, at one point in mind so to speak, in the infinite awareness of the big g*, to begin it all.

It is worth noting here that this image can BE our own mind's eye. We can create the same light within our own inner space. If we close our eyes and focus on the middle point, constantly increasing the focus and intensity, smaller and smaller into a bright white dot. Effectively, the vibration increases to a point of infinite vibration etcetera in the awareness of the big g. In us, that point could be our pineal gland. Slightly above and in front, shaped like a grain of rice or perhaps a soft and squishy Hexahedron?

We could call the first light the seed of creation, or the god particle. Picture it now, in your own minds eye.

Playing a divine frequency will assist in the meditative process. A divine sonic frequency resonating in the background to guide you, in expanding your own individual awareness perhaps? You could try 1080 Hz to begin with.

The awareness of self and the awareness of change created the potential for repetition based on experience. Based on what was realised in the reality of NOW.

With one comes the potential for many, as will and focus create with love based upon desire.

The divine principle of creation is simply, what has been created, can BE created again. The duplication of the divine seed in infinite space creates a new linear dimension.

This duplication is similar to the division of cells, I feel. Two white dots as it were, side by side.

With the existence of the 2 positions we have Dimension. Because with 2 points we can create a line to illustrate the nature of the creation and the potential for infinite linear dimension.

Simply repeating the process again, we see created, a second dimension.

With the existence of three positions, 3 white dots of divine seed, we have the potential of 2 dimensions. Length and width. We see the creation of the Tri-Angle. 3 relationships. If we imagine, 3 small ball shapes of equal size (table tennis balls perhaps), we can see how easily a fourth ball can be added to three, creating the Tetrahedron.

The 3rd dimension is created. Height. And so, Space is created.

Notice the 3 relationships have grown to become 6.

In this 3rd dimension we have space, but not the principle of consciousness.

We haven't got that from which all things come, and to which all things can return.

We need another simple repeated step to create the seed of consciousness in principle.

A simple repetition of the creative principle upon the initial divine seed.

We can now see the simple addition of the fifth element which is the mirror reflection of the fourth element just added It balances the form which, when represented as a geometric structure, displays the Hexahedron. Made of 2 Tetrahedrons. This natural and simple step displays a most natural progression.

Notice the 6 relationships that were 3, have now become (with the addition of the fifth element), 9 relationships.

This is a special structure. It has special properties.

For between Nothing (0), and the 9, we create the Divine Octave, from which all octaves follow!

When I see the creation of the light/love love/light, I see the three spheres in my mind's eye. I can see the cradle, formed where they all join. Here the fourth divine element sits to create the form of a Tetrahedron. On the opposite side of the first three elements, opposite where the fourth sits, we place the fifth element and the harmony is realised in infinite space.

Space is populated by god particles or Divine Seeds.
Fired into being anything by love. Which is the creative force directed by our Will; itself the product of the combination of the perfect harmonic cluster of the 5 Divine Seeds, creating consciousness in potential, which resides as a portal for our awareness to BE, as the expression of an other self, of the ONE.

The energy and frequency of the seed is infinite, yet seemingly nothing; holding within it the infinite potential of all imaginable.

Infinite intelligence in each divine seed. The Principle of Consciousness from the collective of the 5 divine elements in hexahedron form.

The unfolding of the universe displays the growth and ever-changing nature of creation.

Remember that we have labelled as divine seeds, the 5 original components that combine to create the Divine Element for consciousness. Through which vibration is refined to support our awareness, journeying through octaves, each step a further refinement.

Labels are simply an ID for a point of common reference and nothing more.

The single element was created by the focus of the creator's awareness until infinite energy through infinite frequency was achieved.

This process of creation, can be seen as the whole of the

electromagnetic scale. Which is infinite?

The effective breathing, the drawing in/out - up/down of the wave, increasing the speed of wave itself and the energy created until infinite energy and frequency is attained.

Through the creation of all, an awareness of all in potential is evident. The infinite energy has infinite awareness and therefore infinite intelligence to create, The Infinite.

Here again we might pause and consider this all-inclusive label to ID the big g. What is the big g?

The big g is The Infinite.

We can see a demonstration of the innate creative BEing of intelligence in nature when considering the instances of the Fibonacci sequence.

While everyone identifies a pretty curve, have we considered the decision to build in such a way?

Remember, there is no chaos in the repetition of form, created to perpetuate the same, as is.

Does this represent choice? Yes. Through the repeated consistency of the choice itself!

If we journeyed around the rim of the opening, we would become aware of changes in the size of build portion, at needed locations only, to produce a curve like structure!

I don't believe that arcs are a natural form in creation.

Why?

Because to form an arc, we must move matter through a path, determined by a radius who's point of control is potentially unattached and/or unrelated!

Additionally, the mapping of the build stages for say, a shell, would need to be measured, and relationships determined based on a 3-dimensional spread of the build proportions.

I feel more evidence of choice evident as we see a wider distribution of variable choices in build portion perhaps?

We realise a 2D experience and its data is vastly different from a 3D experience and the data related to that.

BE aware that what we perceive is not always necessarily the way things are! Especially now we are aware of the limited sight possessed here.

To help in visualising the divine harmonic cluster, we can zoom in to gain a more expanded awareness.

We can connect the points with lines to demonstrate, to some degree, their spatial relationship with each other. This produces a graphic we may all be more familiar with;

(see youtube video https://youtu.be/bKoECdfq1GA).

When we are familiar, we feel more at ease. When at ease, we absorb more into awareness!

So, space is made up of infinite potential by virtue of the existence in awareness of infinite intelligent energy which is the seed of creation.

The presence of light creates the infinite dark as a potential for infinite light.

From a single manifested point, we extended through repetition to create dimension.

We extended dimensionally to create space.

With infinite space and an awareness of the infinite potential contained therein, we can create anything.

And we can remember how the original focus of the big g's awareness increased the frequency of cycle and the energy to an infinite level to create the god particle (for want of a label), as it were.

Infinite intelligent energy. The divine seed BEcomes a perfectly balanced harmonic cluster of infinite energies, which on a component level, has experienced the creation of all we could perceive, to form what we identify and label as the electromagnetic scale.

The dynamic nature of the 9 relationships of the 5 particles in the divine harmonic cluster, all producing infinite intelligent energy which creates the principle of consciousness harmonically. *Our portoal to this Universe.*

From the creator we get the breath of life, the pulse or the heartbeat of the universe.

It's the zing.

When we consider the scale, it runs through a series of repeating 8's.

Between NOTHING and the divine harmonic cluster (the principle of consciousness) we find the scale. The building block of everything.

Between 0 and 9 we find 1,2,3,4,5,6,7 and 8, the octave. So, we can consider the full effect of the harmonic cluster which means we must include the 9.

123456789 x 9 = 1111111101 which is the Binary achieved, as in the negative and positive energies in addition to everything in the scale.

That which we consider the male +'ve (Positive). The female is -'ve (Negative).

Here we find balance.

All creation in perfect harmonic potential; all contained within the Divine Harmonic Cluster.

"I am that I am. I created everything, and in creating everything I have created you as me in potential, so as to BE with I am.

To BE with I am you must BE as I am. You must grow in awareness of the infinite in potential, to BEcome aware, with the infinite intelligence, and so find the balance within the infinite to experience the bliss that I am."

The big g. 19092021

The structure of the smallest complete created thing remains constant in form, but changes the frequency according to desire.

The full scale manifested in the first point of focus. Giving, the god particle.

We can consider the creation of dimensions. Beginning with the first element and the potential infinite darkness. Then the second element, which is simply a repeat of the experience in awareness of the creation of the first element.

As we see again in the division of the cell, so too appears the second divine element; manifested to sit alongside of the first. Here we have the potential for infinite length. Linear dimension. It creates the potential for infinite distance.

A third element to gain a second dimension. A potential for a change in direction.

Then the fourth element gives us height and the potential for mass.

We can reflect on the structural growth of the divine harmonic cluster, to find the necessary balance within the infinite as we consider purpose.

When we look at the structure, we find a single element which sits within the infinite with no relation to any other thing. We can picture a single table tennis ball perhaps.

A divine element; infinite intelligent energy; as a part of the principle of consciousness in potential.

The second element is created to sit adjacent the first. Think of two table tennis balls super glued together.

The infinite potential for spatial relationship can BE realised as desired.

A third divine element is created, which creates the first perfect harmony. Picture three table tennis balls super glued together.

Again, we can realise the change with the infinite potential of spatial variation.

When we add a fourth element, it is naturally pulled to sit in the cradle of the first three elements created.

A fifth element is created which sits opposite the fourth, and perfect harmonic resonance is created. The 5 elements combined as one to create the principle of consciousness. Stepping 1, 2, 3, 6 and 9.

How the energy changes and in what way, with the addition of the fourth, which is balanced or fully harmonised and changes again as a whole, with the addition of the fifth element is open for speculation.

The dynamic nature of the energies and the relationships between all 5 elements as they each sit in their only possible positions, creates the Divine Harmony. The portal for our Divine awareness to BE *aware!*

Currently of course, with our limited sight we are not fully aware of the wonder of creation. The purpose of this text is to assist in the growth of the awareness of self and the all and what each is and their relationships.

Invisible to our Human eye which has a narrow band of view, the rest of creation observes our changes as we progress through this experience.

~*~

Being god's children, we are all the same.

But as with all children, we grow, we change, we learn and evolve. We raise our vibration, we increase our awareness.

Be aware of the variations in awareness in individuals.

This is not a case of superiority due to the ALL BEing ONE. I am more aware in this individual than another perhaps, yet I am still, that which I am. All other self can be treated, as I am that I am..

The creation of billions of souls.

Each having male and female elements, as a notion perhaps? Yes, it is just a notion. To align with the the sense of duality in all things.

A notion of opposites to bring harmony and balance in unity. For what we may consider male and female is the motion of what we could refer to as the breath of god.

The pulse of life throughout the universe is like the big g drawing in the breath to create the pulse, which then repeats in cycle. The electromagnetic scale, gods breath, draws in to the infinite. Repeats. In, out, in, out, positive, negative, positive, negative, in, out, in, out. Cycle after cycle. Faster and faster. We can pause here. Our breathing reflects the initial creative process.

Consider your breath in meditation, for it is a source of awareness through experience. Look inbetween breath.

As a soul made in the image of our creator, we have no awareness of self here (currently), due to the veil of confusion. This changes on death of the shell or before, if we go through the process of self-resurrection (experience of self beyond the veil of confusion).

Within the womb, at the moment of conception, there is an attachment, as chosen by the soul.

This will be the law of attraction, based on a desire to learn from experiences contained within a particular family/social dynamic.

It involves certain aspects of awareness and specific experience, as agreed, prior to conception.

These experiences are many and varied as the creator chooses to express self into awareness through the direction of freewill, our special gift created by the 'veil of confusion'. Specific behavioural traits are sought to ensure a particular lesson in potential. The expectation is to experience through action and become aware, after which on passing, one can review the experience. We gain awareness of cause and effect by BEing within the experience, and we strive to balance within our awareness using the experience. On the receiving end of all our thoughts words and deeds.

In some instances, a greater awareness is apparent in an individual, which causes a variation in the family line.

Through a change in behaviour based on an awareness of the need for greater self-control, an individual has become aware of the choice available.

The catalyst for this change is a feeling of discomfort or more accurately DIS-HARMONY, which is experienced when an action out of harmony with the desires of the soul is experienced.

To cease the lower vibrational behaviour is the goal through greater self-control based on an understanding, which reflects an expanded awareness, through recognition that the lower vibrational behaviour does not reflect the ONE path.

We must each tame the BEast within, literally!

This initial deception of BEing without an awareness of source allowed the ego of the animal to develop. That sense of self based only on the Beast within, which views only that without!

Understand here, the potential for difference when considering what we perceive as conscious attraction, as opposed to divine intervention, in an automated way as the divine laws of creation are realised. Divine laws are based on cause and effect. When you know what's what, you can choose according to your desired outcome, because you BEcome the creator.

Every moment in awareness is a crossroads. Do x or y. The task is to seek ******* higher vibration always. This IS the ONE Path.

Take the high road.

While Beans remain in cycles of delusion, as truth is laid before them, they cement their future.

Ashes to ashes, dust to dust.

To maintain the notion of freewill according to purpose, freewill must BE just that and nothing less.

It follows, that any energy (vibration/individual awareness), that suppresses, controls or stops the potential for change in another energy (vibration/individual awareness), the controlling energy (vibration/individual awareness), must BE lower in vibration that the targeted level vibration desired, of the energy being suppressed.

This is an extremely negative act. It is also quite sad, because what we can see here is the complete domination of the BEast over the human animal within, which is the ego or sense of self of the BEast. NOT the higher you.

This action can contribute to the removal at some stage of the potential for growth towards the ONE creator. In this way, the creator can infinitely grow in awareness away from self.

This creates that which we think of as evil. That which is devoid of love. That which chooses to move away from the ONE creator.

Here, I repeat the caution.

If you would continue in your awareness towards the ONE, on the one path, you will enjoy the rewards of expanded awareness.

In my awareness, nothing is wasted.
No opportunity for growth.

To get access to a porthole, to enable a step to be taken, only to fail to make the grade as it were,and have to begin at the beginning, again. Going through countless lives it seems; to BEcome more that you were each time, again. Perhaps a little time is well spent. After all, there is much to gain by listening with two ears. There, could be balance found. And growth is just a choice away.

To seek to learn with the veil?

Will that ever be an option again, as the excesses of choice and action, the causing of such extremes that can only get better, to continue in extending the expression in awareness of the creator through experience?

The ongoing nature of growth currently apparent on our planet serves to fuel the movement away from love.

As is the desire of the ONE creator.
However, we must always consider balance.
As we move away from love, we develop our sense of self, based on our blind ego.
Through the ages of this cycle we have witnessed darkness developed to such an extent, to such degrees of negativity, that a need for balance at completion of cycle seems necessary.
So, we see the resurgence of awareness towards the light, as souls (individual awareness (an expression of god's awareness)), choose the opportunity to learn and expand in awareness, in the nature of darkness, to then BEcome aware of the light by choice, and so grow more fully, in a more balanced way.

Note from self - *True Wisdom is undiluted by emotion.*

Wisdom, overcomes all notions of positive and negative in the end, as balance is found through the wisdom in knowing.

The risk here though, is a simple one.
As your soul pushes to increase the intensity of the experience, you can find yourself seemingly stuck in the cycles of the BEast. Laced in the family lines of lies, they all have their quirks and uses. Even towards a darkened excess.
And once again I'm found to muse, their but for the grace of god go I. I am to witness that beginning of end so often speculated, yet so simply formulated.

There is no trick in allowing other self to wallow in the nonsense of a BEast ego. Repeatedly beaten by every weakness, by every trait of excess found in that which is not. Driven by a fear-full, deluded self, a desperate shell.
To grow in the positive, to BEcome aware of the error and

choose to correct it within self, is to re-associate with the path to the ONE.

It is to re-engage with all things Love.

To move away from error where found by individual choice. (A late addition in the back of this book, you will find a piece called "change happens now!").

To BEcome humbled from the realisation of the true nature of self in relation to the whole, and that all expression is the expression of the big g by default.

But that does not discount in any way the nature of this new aspect of creation, and the true debt of the denial of truth.

Through the experience of that which is not, we can become aware of and can choose that which is.

A question of …

To BE, or not to BE? That is the Question.

From this moment in awareness onwards, we have a task; to overcome the errors of our ancestors, which weigh heavy on our souls, by coice.

We have chosen to experience these errors, but must also find the strength to free ourselves from the ties of this cycle, whatever it is.

A family contains error. We wish to learn and experience that particular error, to balance the experience through self-control and understanding. Now or on passing.

Note from self;
To walk a path, is to know an outcome. One path, one outcome.
Stray off the ONE path and you are NOT on ANY path.
Know this!

You can of course, simply recreate the error, which is to echo the failings of the past and set certain, the perpetuation of the error, waiting for another perhaps?

No. This is all about the individual. Your world, your choice. Your learning. So, learn!

One could see them as facilities of experience. To intensify the catalyst of change within.

We can choose to be present. To be real here in the now. To apply love in all things.

We can seek guidance from our soul, our higher self. Seeking guidance from god; in all things.

Receive that guidance in intuition and know your own truth. For ALL truth is within!

The big g is beyond words, and for us, words are truly mightier than the sword, as we have found to our detriment as well as to our advantage.

We simply have to distinguish which is beneficial and which is not.

For the pain of sharp words, from spiteful, viscous and unloving tongues, can destroy the love within. Temporarily of course.

For the purpose of learning, always!

Every action, has a reaction.

This is cause and effect.

Every action has a consequence.

Every unloving act does damage to your soul, or more accurately, lowers your vibe. Every unloving act comes with a price – a lower vibration.

Then there's balance of course. Something to understand as part of an ongoing refinement.

As we meter out torment, we stack up our future pain, and we lower our vibration. This is why we must be true to our heart's desire.

Try to be loving always.

Present, in the moment. Always open to the awareness of wider circumstance.

Ignoring the little voice of ego. That of the beast without!

This is the awareness of self of the human animal, not the higher BEing, the existence of which is known to you already! Call your name within… In the quiet of your inner awareness. Don't give up.

People may search for a soul mate, they may consider that one exists, but we have discussed the creative nature of the big g and already discovered the breath of god is the eternal pulse of the universe, it's heartbeat so to speak. The positive and negative in cycle.

Simply balancing the positive and negative within the self is enough. This awareness relates more to the individual, I feel. The love of our life, and beyond; Eternity? Or simply the different nature of two poles realised?

Behaviour. Action. Do this or that, x or y. Niether is reliant on the other for an expanded awareness of self.

To BE, is to create as you Will!

To recap.

This journey is about expanding individual awareness with experience based completely on freewill. Essentially, we raise our vibration by making positive choices.

If we make negative choices we lower our vibration.

Now, with the suggested completion of the master cycle, we have two potential outcomes, I feel.

In this experiment of creation employing the veil of confusion as a means of creating powerful catalyst for change, I believe the destructive nature of BEast in potential could be harnessed and contained, and may need to be. For what is created cannot BE uncreated.

We also know that one thing can influence another thing. The one thing can change the nature of another.

So, a need for the containment of destructive energies, some dimensional space where the creation of ever decreasing levels of vibration is realised, would assist in the creator extending the experience of self perhaps? As a part of a balancing process for all other self.

So, if you choose to stay as you are, you may BEcome a part of a growing and ever decreasing source of negative energy. One which is contained so as to not contaminate, influence or change in any way, energy that is choosing to stay on the path to ONE.

This suggests an increase in the notion of balance also.

It certainly contains the potential and expectation of an increasing negative energy; suggesting what some may consider an uncomfortable existence as we relate from this perspective and experience, now.

Hell.

Stop behaving like an animal, and BEgin by acting like a god in potential. Humble, as you are aware of the power in potential within.

Fearless, as you know and understand, and so simply accept and make divine awareness-based choices for the good of you and other self.

"Now you have a chance, they whispered."

2 choices, ONE outcome. All becomes a part of all that is eventually … silly Beans.

~*~

There's talk of science cutting off the big g, but science is the big g!

It's all just evolution in awareness… everything evolving.

Changing in awareness. Even if it's only round and round a cycle. Subtle variations are always evident.

We can't prove the colour of a dinosaur's body, but it did have a colour.

We can't prove a big bang took place, but we can embrace the notion of a single point of origin based on the trajectories of all things moving away from it. Can we determine the source

or amount of energy required to cause a bang this big?
So many questions. Infinite questions? Of course.
We can't prove the evidence of love, but we believe in love.
We feel it, if we're lucky (when we know what it truly is).
Science is the study of all things created, nothing more, nothing less.
Science can be creative,
and likewise, can also be destructive.
The notion of evil is born of the human animal.
Its bed is one of fear and dysfunction through disharmony.
Its fuel is the torment of self, in endless cycles of despair.
Casting our eyes to yesterday, we can see from the early beginnings how the Bean could view the sun as god.
It brings light and warmth.
Makes us feel comfortable and content.
Similarly, dark thunderous skies with flashings of lightning could cause fear, concern and confusion in the awareness of early humankind.
In the very cradle of this awareness of self, fear through unknowing was realised.
The notion of good and bad is simply derived from comfort or discomfort.
Based on feelings from action, reflecting the emotions of the Bean. The Human BEan. The Human Animal. The BEast. 666.
Slowly through the process of growth, an awareness of feelings came to awareness. Something new; reasoning based on more than just the immediate demands of the survival of me, our only point of reference.
Directing action, as in whether to act or not. Based on reason. Expanded reason. All from observations and reflections on the 4 Actions.
Action by us affecting self.
Action by us affecting outside of self.

Action by other affecting us.
Action by other affecting other.
Applying a notion of comfort or discomfort to any of the four action states above, serves to fuel our fight or fligt responses. This is the baseis for decision making in the human animal, the BEast. Learninng from our environment what is dangerous and what isn't we build a world of comfort.
With time, simple feelings and actions give way to complex thoughts, rationalisations, what ifs, and with thought came a more imagined fear and ego; and so, we began creating imagined error!
When did the first parents arrive? How does this fit in with the evolved?
Were the first parents simply those that were physiologically developed to such an extent that the soul/awareness could manifest to the point of awareness of the same within the individual? This is an ongoing truth for all.
Time will unfold all before us, as we desire, on an individual level. Such is the nature of awareness.
To expand each moment just a little more. To consider it all over and over. This is the greatest awareness to ponder after all!
There is a seeker within all of us. Some just sleep. Some are waking. Some are rubbing their eyes in disbelief.
But we all have the potential to seek and find that which we most desire. What we yearn for with a burning passion deep in our awareness.
The sad truth is that humankind has deteriorated on a soul awareness level.
Through the constructs of our minds, we have weaved a web of lies and deceptions, of self-delusions; to the point where there appears no winner. For the actions of some do no more than move us further away from the big g.
Fooling themselves with a totality that amazes the aware!

And to what end is this pursued? That may be to hell. We all have choice. Choice and Intent can BE changed at any moment, to save yourself from so much more; we begin by choice, to think, to accept; why would it not be so? It could BE so; and were it so then yes, we are immortal. The awareness lives on.

There are many deceptions here in this awareness, and unloving intent runs rampant through the hallways of Business, Government and Religion, as indeed it always has.

The human bean has lost sight of many truths along the way. Empires come and go. Civilisations come and go.

PLANETS for learning, come and go!

Catalyst to bring change, will always come as needed.

"Look what I do…" well it's done, to, be 'cause' of more.

("See, even the pawns begin to wake and see!").

Every, thing and everyone has purpose because there is always interaction.

~*~

The single greatest power in the known expanse, that would be love

To deny this is to be unaware of the true creative power of love.

It is the ultimate force; the only force for change.

This truly identifies the potential of destructive and constructive power available.

This also ensures limitation in expansion through an inability to proceed due to current vibration.

Consider this all you will, to determine truth.

The journey of your existence in the awareness that you are, is in a literal sense, based on the form you aspire to. which is a process of continuous growth in awareness, including periods of stagnation.

For in each cycle of stagnation, learning repeatedly takes place until a shift up in vibration is achieved.
Remember…

I AM THAT I AM! And that would BE YOU!

It can drive one to despair and destruction, or when balanced, towards natural or divine love (a love that is unconditional).
A place of bliss and contentment through knowing. The best foundation to build on.
It will create all things of wonder and benefit *to those that would listen* to their own desires and follow the search for the truth in your passions.
It is the driving force behind all human life.
The single spark of all life and knowing; present in every cell, in every known living thing.
All that is animated in some way however slight.
All beans are created equal in the eyes of the big g, and should be viewed the same by all beans. All other notions are born of a childlike awareness, which is born of the BEast, the human animal.
Fear Greed Envy etcetera,
When we cast our eyes judgmentally over another, we divert our own attention away from our self.
In this way, we can avoid finding and having to correct error within ourselves.
To judge the reflection in the mirror takes courage and honestly.
To focus on oneself with a view to growth, is to be free to exercise your will to create according to your passions and desires.
To do this with a bias towards love and the service and benefit of all other self, is to seek and find the greatest rewards.
The more noble the task the better.

The Bigger - The Bolder - The Better.

It is a matter of Honour and Duty to self to aspire to all you could perceive to BE, in the nature of the big g.

Consider the earth, the planet, our home.

Natural – full of Nature.

A living organism teaming with biodiversity, the likes of which could drive one mad at the complexity of it all.

We live here. It is our home.

But do we know our place?

If we were truly aware of our real importance in the eyes of our creator, and the total lack of importance in the grand scheme of things, would we act less destructively perhaps?

How is such evil evolving?

Please be aware, I do not believe in evil per se, as everything in awareness is based on perspective which reflects the journey of the individual awareness.

Catalyst comes into our awareness in varying ways to assist in the process of growth. Growth is raising your awareness/vibration.

It is in the nature of the catalyst in experience that things develop to intensify the experience in our awareness. This notion is highly specific to our current awareness.

Is it necessary for us to evolve on a human level as well?

Of course!

To evolve into an awareness of love as a creative force is the ultimate goal. When fully aware of the creative power of love, you can begin to create in powerful ways using love as the force to create.

To evolve in our awareness of the human animal that is in effect our host in a slightly abstract way.

To evolve mentally in increasing awareness, which is simply our thoughts.

Increasing awareness can lead to the awareness of the divine human.

When the awareness of your divine nature has come down, so to speak, to sit within your awareness as you walk this earth; that's you, BEing in this world, but not of this world.
For thousands of years humankind has evolved.
Within that sense of evolving, freedoms were curtailed to some degree, as controls began over many. An expanded or greater sense of self in some, the ego of the BEast, contributed to this notion of control to overcome fears. It was a part of the development of the ego within the BEast itself.
The fight for survival as part of the natural processes here on this planet, led to this development and a sense of superiority developed by those in control. They achieved their positions of control by guile, cunning and brute strength, displayed in the murdering of an opponent who challenged the top position.
Ultimately, a lineage of power, taken under false pretences.
Time after time after time.
The claim for superiority, driven by the ego and nothing more.
There are no foolish households, royal or otherwise.
All realise the fragility of their own positions, and the lies that bolster the farce that constitutes their very existence. That each and all involved believe they can alleviate the burden of self-growth;
or worse still, there is no belief in a requirement for the individual to evolve.
Houses came and went as they always do.
Individual/family or national identity.
All the same, all based on the nonsense of fear and survival.
The biggest fool is the fool that fools oneself!
With inequality came resentment.
With judgement came resentment.
With fear came resentment.
With anger came resentment.
With guilt came resentment

The guilt came from death.

From murderous acts. The taking of life.

Which gave birth to the need and search for justification in those actions observed by others.

Guilt, Shame, Hatred, Anger, Violence and Death. Feelings of destruction within.

And so, the seeds of destructive repetition were planted and developed over time.

Repeated in self or others, through the lines of birth, of lineage. Error echoed through the generations. Echoing to this very day.

To offer those necessary opportunities for growth in awareness through experience.

As thought/awareness creates everything, everything is somewhere. In another time/space. A moment, created in mind, explored, and captured in another space/time dimension perhaps?

Then on passing, one finds so much balance in awareness as we embrace the truth of creation.

Or, if we find ourselves surrounded by low vibration, we can begin to think of the big g. Think of the light of creation. Of what we are in potential. That everything is a choice and a decision can BE made at any time or place.

Just knowing, is enough to kick start your realignment on the ONE path.

Hell, 'The Inferno', may be, as Dante's dream, a place to move through with haste should you ever find yourself there.

A place for people to dwell as their personal energy/vibration reduces.

Somewhere safe to store that which is stuck in a low vibratory cycle.

Appreciate the creator's position towards the individual, the total of other self to ONE, when ONE is ALL.

You are awareness within a confined space, developed to

allow the growth of the individual.
If the individual does not grow, that is the choice of the individual, as perceived.
As you believe, so shall it BE.
Now realise the deflection of blame towards the big g for what it is. The simple shifting of blame. Such nonsense.
We are supposed to do it all here ourselves. If this aligns with your personal hopes, give in to truth IF you want to. Accept the truth and realise – difference! Know, the same.

~*~

Here, we pause and marvel at the good things, for there is much to be in awe of!
Here, we begin to see our creator in the flesh as it were. And we reference back to previous pages where we examine the creation of space.
The creation of the first divine element. The first breath of the big g.
It reminds me of the first gasp of life a baby takes on having the bottom slapped.
The creation of the divine seed through the combining of the first 5 elements.
At this point I pause to consider the effect of having infinite intelligent energy combined. The principle of consciousness created; the notion of BEing aware and responsive to one's surroundings.
I AM THAT I AM
The notion of creation. That creation took place with the first change.
With the first movement in awareness. Movement in dimension.
That through repeated cycles and the focussing of awareness

on BEing, which is outside of the awareness itself, is where the first movement was created inside the awareness of self. In a space, created for the purpose of its existence and that first movement. Then a repetition of the same, until…we get history.

"In the beginning was the Word, and the Word was God."

And so, we see the first glimpse of all that is.
To grasp the notion of an infinite intelligence, of infinite awareness, able to focus on a single point in awareness, with an infinitely increasing frequency, achieved by the focus of the creative force that is love, as passion, desire, intention, expectation, acceptance and gratitude keep reading.
A notion expanded upon to an infinite point in existence. To the extent that it BEcomes all that is, *in that awareness*.
All created for the single purpose of knowing self and growth of other self, through expanding awareness; found through experience in what is created as other self!
All created within the infinite intelligence of infinite awareness that created the notion of a universe as part of a multiverse, within a varying dimension, of that which is OMNI in all aspects of its nature as…
The Infinite ONE. God.
The big g.
Life. All life.
Every notion of existence, created in a cycle of continuous change, evolving, growing, improving, progressing.
All part of a master plan by someone called the big g.
A plan derived from will.
Will is a creative desire – control deliberately exerted, upon love, the fuel of change. So change occurs.
A will that is unrestrained to ensure the fullest exploration of infinite growth in awareness.

We know this at this time in our awareness as free will. Choice.

Free will is the single most important aspect of this awareness. *To deny the free will of another is a major error in that it affects your vibration so negatively. The control achieved, is the opposite of the purpose here.*

The prime purpose here, is to experience love by means of total free will, choice. In all we appear to do.

To express, boundless will through awareness as the ultimate goal perhaps!

To be guided as children and not controlled, that is the challenge. To allow the expression of free will in awareness under guidance.

Around the age of 13, we begin to BEcome more aware.

This is when we can be introduced to the notions of an inside awareness where it has not been considered already. Also, the notion of training self with a view towards self-resurrection, so as to walk on the earth but not BE of the Earth.

To walk as the Divine Human - BEing guided by Divine Awareness.

As babies, we encounter mistake and error at every turn.

It is all we know. It is how we learn.

Yet in every tiny measure of time (the passing of moments as awareness), we experience change and growth as a constant.

For change is the single constant for all life.

It is truly all we know.

Nothing stands still. Creation is always moving.

Fearless babies embracing all from day one of the veiled awareness.

Deviating from the norm is truly only momentary, as we change the focus on new cycles of awareness, born of the sensory feedback from our 5 basic senses.

In this natural world of conscious feedback, we are introdu-

ced to a new form of awareness. An awareness of intensified experience through the notion of such things as pain, in the biodiverse shell that is our body. Of *feeling* alone.
In this way, we progress beyond each learning opportunity/ experience, changing all the while.
Adapting to our new world.
Focussing on survival. Fitting for a beast wouldn't you say?
The single reason we have become detached from the big g is because it was engineered to be so. To increase the intensity of the catalyst that is a part of the process, which speeds the excesses in behaviour and thereby the learning (the re-assessment of the life experienced, on passing/death).
Our relationship with the big g is a singularly personal one. Strictly for the individual.
It has nothing to do with any church or so-called house of god, although these can be used in freewill, to focus upon your relationship with the big g, ONLY where there is NO DOGMA, derived from man's envy, greed and lusts.
Your salvation is by the individual, as in you alone, for the individual (you), that's it.
Going to church and singing once a week pays no attention to the learnings of the soul, rather the repeating cycle of dependency upon another through fear of failure perhaps or simply not growing up to meet your responsibilities?

"Help me Jesus!" (Really? Still?).

A perception of evil (which equates to some form of non-compliance), is where salvation is thought to be needed. When in truth we are simply talking about the extension of the experience here and now. Based on nothing more than personal choice.
Many lives have been taken in the names of different rulers of one kind or another. Here is where we must consider the

SYSTEM.

We have talked of this earlier, but will consider things in slightly different ways.

Truth is simply Natural Law and Divine Law.

It is a truth that the sun radiates heat and light, based on our awareness, sensory observations and personl experience.

That water evaporates to form clouds; and in turn, waters the surface of the Earth to encourage life through growth in some way.

The human animal as experienced, is a bio-electrical-mechanical entity here on Earth.

Yet truly we are more than this.

When we think, we create waves of energy which can be measured.

Energy can create forms.

Energy promotes change, the basis for all growth within the Universe.

Consider the notion of the hells.

The Hells are created with all negative low frequency unloving energy created by the thoughts, words and actions of those that remain trapped in this place, in cycles of blind torment. Here we balance our awareness through the experience of all we did as recipient! It is through the experiencing of our actions upon others that we find the balance in our awareness. So we know both the giving and receiving anything.

Judge not, lest ye be judged. Kill not, lest ye be killed etcetera. YOU set your future awareness and the path of discovery contained therein.

I will come back to our true form and BEing/Nature/Experience later.

The law of attraction suggests in its essence that like attracts like.

However, we should remember the front of the book…

"It is NEVER a question of 'that which you desire, I deliver unto thee', No.
It is simply a case of such as YOU DESIRE, YOU deliver unto SELF"
(the big g)

The universe is an infinitely intelligent resource.
That some begets more and more begets much. Creation is always moving.
This itself suggests an accumulation of energy, whether positive or negative, which is all down to perspective and personal disposition one could say; choice/free will.
Is being attracted to the realm of the Hells an indicator of negative thought waves?
Are the Hells a place where we experience 'payback', as it were?
For we are the sole creators and masters of our own fate!
So yes, *one could consider the hells as paying us back to provide balance in awareness through experience.*
Due to the choices made here, being responsible for all received there, the burden of choice remains with the exerciser of the free will. Blame can only be apportioned to self; so the ramifications of behaviour should now be clear. A punishing hand, a deathly blow.
Creations of the fight or flight mechanism.
The measure of anger, hatred, and evil as perceived within oneself, is the measure we should be aware of, with a view to change here and now! Else, we might expect to experience the Hells in some form, receiving our just deserts, learning from our error, when we get to where we go on passing.
Behaviour, is the single measure of man/woman/BEan.
All words are projections here, unless completely alone with no listeners.
All thoughts serve to express all that you can BE. To explore

the notion of limitless creation. Deeds done upon another, fall due in some way, at some place in some moment of your awareness to gain balance.

The story on the grapevine runs that Julius Caesar spent one thousand years in pain. To find balance.

Acute, severe, real pain. As he chose to have metred out to all before him.

Imagine that. The notion of constantly ripping open flesh to produce pain, to balance things within awareness through experience. Personal experience.

The experience there is felt, just as here. Awareness is awareness after all!

And from this experience we have all the sensory input of a seemingly timeless experience.

All this pain in awareness and experience for a thousand years or more?

There's a thought! It makes one consider based on a new understanding perhaps? Understanding that balance is always found. *That we, you or I, all in fact, always have a choice. To end some thing, some way, some sense of being, and experiencing. To bring change and growth.*

After experiencing all the physical and subsequent emotional pain, and having spent his quest on all he had personally chosen to accumulate, Julius Caesar heard about another way. He wondered of different things. It was then that he turned to the light.

He was guided towards the truth.

This is how he began the very personal and individual journey of change, as he chose to walk towards the big g.

This journey is ongoing of course; as it is for all of us, until it isn't.

Remember, as a major cycle finishes, all life will cease.
To close off the cycle, the planet will no longer support life.
Know what this means, and why all should get their own

houses in order!

Awareness to a higher level than this density will pass on, up. Those that vibrate on lower vibrations will begin again, from the very beginning perhaps, to experience all they did.

Joining a new major cycle somewhere in the universe, once balance is found through polarization, positive or negative.

It is perhaps for this single reason that I remind all of deeds unanswered with respect to balance in awareness!

We can always seek to BE more aware and change behaviour, seeking repentance, forgiving self. Forgiving others to find balance and lose the torment of the anger and revenge cycles that weigh us down.

To project externally is to ignore the internal that craves your attention.

That needs to be observed for you to grow.

To ensure your own growth through change towards new, continues.

Errors are then corrected if that is your choice. Or one can continue to explore a particular direction.

Here I'm referring to the notion of negative energy within self.

To lose control of yourself is to become too invested in this world. Too invested in the ego of the human beast. Too bogged down in negative cycle.

To pause in your awareness, to stay in the present, is to evaluate and assess your current position, your thoughts as they present themselves literally, and if you so choose, you can take on a course of corrective action, as circumstance presents. To get back on track maybe; feeling content and back in control. Fearless even. This is as easy as saying stop!

Then changing your relationship with some thing or someone or some situation or circumstance, through new action, your action, which influences all around you in some way.

This is change, growth and progress. It's good.

We are always responsible for all we do, not the big g. We need to remember that!

The SYSTEM is one of perfection and utter simplicity. It is simply based on constant change, of all created, to infinitely expand awareness of self, through experience of other self in infinite forms and based on infinite stimuli.

Part of which is our awareness in experience; any and all experience of all of humankind, over all time.

The expansion of awareness with increasing intensity is born of the veil of confusion.

For there is no way of getting away from the truth and simplicity of what simply IS.

This is a very dynamic extension to the ongoing experiment that is the big g extending the notion of self through growth, in any and all ways including awareness as other self, and that other self, perceiving self as independent of that which created all. This is a perception of the BEast within.

The human bean is the extension of the expression of the big g, within self, by self, for self. We have total freewill and in this experience, always will have. It is only after this life experience, preparing for the next level of awareness, that full realisation of your own awareness is regained; unless of course you self-resurrect (gain an awareness of your immortal self), rather quickly.

The human bean is always responsible for all things in your own awareness. Consider that for a while; it may prove to be mind expanding one could say.

The system had to be this way, otherwise we would be subjugated by the awareness of the big g based on a notion of eternal security and an existing oneness already BEing. Because we simply are.

How could this occur?

Simply by the presence in our awareness of all-encompassing love and peace as a constant. Knowing our immortal self.

The overwhelming nature of the force (Love), of divine love (Divine Force), could distort our rationale for developing faith and love towards the big g, which is growing as we are supposed to.

Such are the workings of idolisation towards that which we perceive as all powerful I feel.

Do we act through love or fear?

To enable us to understand the nature of creation, which in turn allows us to peak at the essence in nature of our creator, we must use and share the same processes for creating our own awareness.

This is, after all, what children do isn't it? Generally, we emulate our parents. Which is why we could try to eradicate cycles within family or society. Create a place of bliss and joy, a playground for the expression of free will through the cooperation of all Beans towards the single goal of maximum personal spiritual development here and now, and so for always.

The need for faith is intrinsic to our nature (in this experience/awareness), to our essence, and the process of creation.

We are free to do literally anything.

But it is good to be aware i.e. mindful, of all potential effects and outcomes of our actions. Especially when another could perceive our actions as unloving, through a sense of misunderstanding or a lack of "Expanded Awareness", to whatever extreme.

That a human bean would measure out (project) judgement, or severe and/or brutal punishment, on a fellow human bean is anathema to the very core of all love.

It displays nothing more than a complete lack of awareness regarding the true sense of purpose, here found!

It is easy for any one of us to unknowingly project negative energy into present awareness. We must guard our thoughts words and deeds always.

To punish or inflict pain or suffering on a child...
here lies a heavy burden, where you lose self-control, based on a lack of awareness of the nature of the cycles that we constantly have the potential to get exposed to and embroiled in.
Respect life.
All life.
Love life.
All life.
The saying, "do unto others as you would have others do unto you", is not just about behaving in a loving way.
Much more than that, it displays or reflects the level of truth and understanding in that awareness; suggesting balance or not as the case may be.
To judge and award the outcome of your own judgement, is as bad as the act of the punishment itself, which is balanced against the action that is being judged. Here may be found little difference, I feel.
Such was the balance Caesar experienced. Which ultimately brought greater awareness.
The simpler the system the less there is to break.
There are no malfunctions in this system.
The perfect system; a self-regulating justice based on choice.
There seems no warning, just truth?
As ye sow, so shall ye reap!

.
...
......
....

Abracadabra

Today

So, is life just a question of birth & survival until death?
Currently, one might say so.
Certainly, it seems that way for the vast majority of beans on the planet.
There seems little time or inclination to gaze inwardly.
Yet this is where we can find many things to improve our lives.

Wherein lies the responsibility for our actions?
So often with others, many believe, or due to circumstance perhaps, as we lack the courage to own our mistakes, which all have roots in our own choices.
There is error around us all from day one.
But we shouldn't feel disheartened, for error as we know is how we learn.
In fact, why not erase the word "error"?
Why not simply refer to 'off path action' and 'on path action'?
Because when we come down to base factors, we just have 2 possible actions, which are either;
action you would do on the path or action you would not do on the path.
Any action can BE loving, truly. But only one action of the two considered would be on the path to ONE.
This makes life and all the choices available, simple to negotiate.
Perhaps more importantly, having chosen this path, growth in awareness grows in a seemingly exponential way.
It is a part of every facet of creation.
It is a part of what we call evolution.
It is part of the process of expansion in awareness.
Every error is progress.
Whether a forward step or a backward step.
Nothing is wasted.
For there is much to be learnt.

How much?

An infinite amount, of course!

The journey itself, towards enlightenment (awareness of your immortal self), is itself a simple step, realised on passing or before. Becoming at one with the ONE takes countless moments in awareness.

Excitement awaits the real seeker. The brave and the true alike.

Which could be all of us perhaps?

It is always all of us, of course!

View error as instantly spent. For all error is progress after all.

Error is worth its weight in gold.

Error is discovery, it is the creation of potential as invention.

Error is creative as a part of the evolutionary process.

It is change.

As a part of our evolution, it's something that…

WE ALL DO!

Do not judge others.

Do not judge yourselves.

For if error is progress, why would you?

BEcome aware of error. Once aware of error, you can take steps to avoid it yourself. That's progress.

To work a lifetime without a moment for internal reflection, is to move forward without direction.

Ultimately, there is but one direction on one path. That path, is the divine path.

Please pause here…

Consider if you will, the discomfort felt by the majority, when the talk turns to,

god

love

self-responsibility

faith

life and death

immortality

The current paradigm is one of management with money.
It has a view towards total control through debt,
to ensure compliance is achieved.
The single basis for this is fear.
Fear of much - felt by many.
This is playing on the true nature of the BEast within. The fear over the notion of survival or death.
Projected by the power, the masses absorb the fear.
The single biggest deception is the need for money.
We live in a world of abundance, and sharing this abundance will make us happy and 'FEARless'! Money is the way by which the chains of slavery are welded to our hearts and souls.
Many deceptions and untruths exist.
It is possible however, to work within the monetary system to remove it, and replace it with some other notion – service to all and self perhaps, as part of one global co-operative mind set.
This for me is the only true way forward!
But what is truth?
Truth is something that resonates with us as individuals, on a very deep internal level.
In the same way that we identify love and fear within ourselves.
We're talking about feelings.
Just the same as the feelings of love that anyone can feel, we can also realise feelings of guilt.
We can harbour feelings of self-loathing, of being unworthy.
These are not loving of self or other self, and as such, have no place in our head-space.
Yet all negative thoughts exist somewhere, in someone's head-space. This is just balance.
The many deceptions as error, we hold onto, will not go

without reward.
For as we have established,
as ye sow, so shall ye reap.
We must think of this in the truest sense of the word, as we create our own realities in our own awareness, moment, by moment.
All deeds not in accordance with love, accumulate as a personal weight around one's neck.
Is it sad that the full weight of realisation comes in - without reference? Unexpected, as we pass through the hells?
If indeed that is where 'our' law of attraction has sent us.
By choice perhaps?
Remember then, that we can change, if it is our desire to do so.
It is, after all, what we do best.
One could say with supreme accuracy that it is all we do, as nothing stays the same in the reality of our awareness.
That and making mistakes of course, as part of process.
All via action and interaction, as we become fired by the catalysts before us.
All realised in our awareness, which we identify as thought.

. ...

Abracadabra.
To exist, is not to live.
One could observe how it suggests the continuing interaction with a cycle; repeating over and over again.
To exist, is not to love.
Not in the sense of increasing one's power through the exploration of your own creative force found within. With which you fashion creation in your reality, as a creator.
Ever expanding your own perceived awareness, which is a tiny part of the whole infinite awareness of the ONE.
To exist, is not to evolve, in the truest sense of our understanding of the word, in its most expansive example.

Simply because, if we do not respond to the catalysts as provided, our reason for being here, learning and growing as we do, is not achieved, potentially. In these final moments of opportunity. It's like not graduating or finishing the course. Not taking it all the way.

One could consider that the human bean decays, in error. Though instantly we are aware that all energy of creation simply evolves, as in, it changes to another form of energy. As we know, change is constant, however perceived, within any potential time reference.

This may seem contradictory regarding the individual, but in truth, all around the individual awareness we find yet more individual awareness, which appreciates constant change as we do. So, the mix of the total infinite potential in infinite awareness is always infinite change. Regardless of whether we do or do not perceive it. Which is always subject to the potential for infinite change; as is any aspect of awareness.

Individual correction is required through choice, by exercising the free will, to save ourselves from our own error. Which is the constant embrace of the cycle, devoid of the necessary acceptance and expanding awareness, approaching balance.

I cannot believe, that our evolution or annihilation should be left in the hands of a few misguided egoists. So, it won't be. For in the sequence of space/time unfolding, we see the nature of some purposed towards the deliverance if you will, of the ending of cycle for countless millions, as we embrace the notion of new in potential.

These seemingly misguided egoists serve a purpose as do all, while they struggle with the errors of the child's mind.

They are lost in their own self-deceptions. Deceptions decided on before, to facilitate the ending of the great cycle perhaps? In the end, there is purpose found in all things.

Ultimately, wisdom will correct all; even if it takes a few billion years for an individual.

The individual must be free. Free to explore self.
Free to decide all things in awareness.
Free to choose that which we focus on.
Free to act, extending that same focus!
Based on nothing more than free will.
Too many beans live in fear.
Too many beans compromise values through fear.
Fear of loss;
of job,
money,
health,
happiness,
freedom,
life itself!
A society that constrains, constrains itself.
It suffocates and destroys the creativity necessary for the expansion and evolution of the whole.
If we cannot be free, free to express ourselves, the glorification of self in expression can only be in black or white so to speak.
Yet colour is who we are, is what we are, as opposed to monotone.
Colour is all around us.
It is a part of us.
Just as we are a part of it.
In nature.
In our home.
This earth, our current playground.
Talking in love, brings colourful expression. An expression that is more expansive than when we simply talk in black and white.
Living in love,
brings a colourful life.
A life to be observed and perhaps reflected upon, as it too is

more expansive than when we live in black and white.
Sleeping in love, excites the soul.
Searching within excites the soul.
Talking to yourself, your true self, creates new possibilities as we expand our expectations of self, always seeking, more.
The very nature of your creative power, love. Based on desire and intention.
Soul; the image of our creator. Our mother and father, god.
The big g that is always simply there as ourselves to guide as requested.

For when we reach out, we always find that which we need at that very moment.

We respond to ourselves based on the potential for awareness within the beast, as it were.
You are, someone that loves you. You are, someone that will always help you.
You, will always provide solutions, as required, to ensure the necessary change, as intended, in all things perceived. This is why, necessity is the mother of invention.
Guidance, from a loving perspective, can be nurtured by you for you.
Therefore, to deny ourselves the opportunity of growth in awareness, now seems unloving in itself, towards self.
To consider that some, potentially many, may dismiss without consideration, the content here recorded.
Recorded for no other purpose save the expansion of awareness in potential or even realised in any and all.

I pray their truth is revealed to them.

Yet, instantly I have to recognise the element of hope and expectation for all, knowing that some are simply not in a place to consider such knowing.
But then, some are. You choose for you!
To dismiss as mere luck, the base notion that we are simply here in awareness, for no rhyme nor reason.

The fact that all that is simply here in our awareness, is just a part of all that is, is a part of awareness itself. Something else to become aware of.

To become aware of these things, is it just a chance occurrence? NO.

It is something to BE embraced as soon as you can begin to consider the notions as potential truths in your awareness.

Can we really choose here and now, as you read these very words, just choose to embrace a new truth? A new awareness; one that has expanded?

Changed?

Yes, of course we can. BE cause, we are all that we want to BE. Always.

One might consider all this to be unimaginable or it might even become a fearful view.

But why should this be so?

To embrace all that truly is, is to be courageous and free.

To live with timidity;

to cling to the norm;

to turn away from truth;

through fear of alienation, within community perhaps?

Here we find another example of compromising our values, based on the cycles that anchor so many beans.

Like…

all the puppets we know of.

Compromising their own values due to fear.

Doctors, journalists, politicians, employees in different companies.

All governments?

Full of beans jostling for position in a fantasy of ego and envy, and nothing more.

The list, sadly, seems endless.

When we consider our values,

let us consider the earth, our home, as perceived.

Here is a gift, a playground for love to grow and blossom like the flowers on a tree as it prepares to give birth to fruit.

When we consider how we ravage and plunder the very essence of that which it is.

Without thought or regard for the future it seems, and it's all driven by greed and money, driven by nothing more than the perception of self within a few.

A few small minds trapped within the never-ending cycle of their own egos.

Lives of individuals are not important to the big money it often seems.

In some ways of course, one could see it all as a part of process, which it truly is of course.

Countless millions of people suffering as part of a dream of service to self.

Yet in truth, with change comes new perspectives, new considerations and reasonings, as the notion of the greater good solidifies within mind and countless millions find service to others and service to self.

As we lose the notion of self, as the ego of the BEast dissolves through an expansion in awareness.

Consider then, the sowing and reaping to come, for all who FAIL to change, to grow, to expand their own notion of self beyond that of human animal based ego!

More cycles of the same perhaps, for lessons learned lead to yet more lessons as the truth dances before your very awareness.

For any, and all, who see human life, any life, as expendable and worthless, is caught up in the most unworthy cycle of self-deceit.

A cycle that can exist for thousands of years perhaps. All subject to personal choice and freewill.

The warnings cannot be given strongly enough.

Not in the sense of right and wrong, for no such thing exists,

as all experience is valid with regard to learn/teach, and teach/learn. Each finding its own balance.
No. The warnings are given over the sense of loss of opportunity to grow on the ONE path!
One could consider that these are journeys of personal growth, based on the notion of cycle, but all we see is self-deception, in various forms.
Greed, lust, avarice,
Denial, guilt, shame,
Frustration, anger, hatred.
Let us not forget the notion of REVENGE.
Such a sturdy lock it is.
Trapping for countless time, the self, within a cycle of despair.
For no growth can be found here.
And so, we begin to understand the power found in forgiveness?

At any time,
one can stop and pause.
One can be present in the now and observe all circumstance.
One can be honest with self. Admitting errors and false beliefs. Delusions of error. Acknowledge projections as error.
Admitting error to self can be hard for the self, for you and for me. For us.
Or it can be easy of course. Simple?
You, make it as easy or as difficult for yourself as You choose, always.
As you desire and wish it to be perhaps?
Here and now, you can be ever present, in the truth of learning, and begin to grow, and simply begin to change your awareness. Go…
From birth, our lives are one of constant error and correction through experience.
We are aware of cause and effect internally.

As we become more proficient with movement, grasping, walking, controlling, physically, we become adept at controlling our interaction with our environment.

All this and so much more takes place.

This is a natural process.

It is one that continues for all our time here.

It is itself, part of a cycle that we explore as we interact with new.

Our physical condition changes according to our desires.

Often, choices are made to our detriment, as we ignore the needs of our environment and circumstance.

Through selfish, and what one could call the irresponsible behaviour of others, we begin to grow in an ever-increasing environment of toxicity.

Embracing the truth in all aspects in relation to our environment and personal nature, will lend itself to forgiveness of self.

Through simply accepting and forgiving, we can correct our behaviour, as we rediscover our true values and core beliefs, our renewed love of self in a positive way.

Then we can consider, what is the truth regarding unconditional love?

We embrace the simple notion of BEing, of having faith in our own beliefs and desires.

Beginning to know truth, we can then gauge ourselves as we begin to grow.

Unconditional love is in the value of giving, without the expectation of anything returned.

It is displayed in simply taking pleasure in another's happiness.

It is beyond tolerance.

Beyond compassion.

It is more than simple empathy.

Unconditional love applies to our self as much as towards all other other self.

It is a position to grow from, as we incorporate the notion of what it is, into our life and into our awareness.

To love is to soar, to be free, to fly high.

It is to seek an understanding of, and love the notion of, the big g.

Love the planet here and now. Love all life.

Love yourself.

We love all human beans because we understand the potential frailty in awareness.

We all have the potential for error!

To observe actions that are not loving is to see truth in awareness.

We must strive to try to understand the motivations behind unloving actions as displayed by others and of course, ourselves.

In this way, empathy can come easily into our awareness as we consider the actions of our self and others.

So often, society dealivers judgement, punishment and treatment to individuals and families of a kind and nature that is… simply error.

Power corrupts

Ego deceives

I this.

I that.

Is it all about I?

Me, me, me perhaps?

This position is simply a desperate state of survival. A struggle to be heard at any cost, in a world full of people that don't seem to care?

Full of fear and lacking a true understanding of love!

We can consider others before self.

We can be generous in spirit.

Projection is simply avoidance ("people in glass houses..." comes to mind).
Are we all in glass houses?
NEVER judge.
Simply accept and try to understand and find empathy.
"There, but for the grace of god (awareness), go I".
When you understand this, you will be on the path of awakening to truth I feel.
Seek unconditional love in all things in your awareness.

~*~

Our home is the planet we have labelled earth.
It is a system of inter-dependence.
Of balance.
Of natural design and growth born of love or logos.
The phrase, 'the strongest *will* survive', references the animal or strength of desire born in awareness.
It can be aligned to the beast within ourselves or the other self that always serves us?
One could say that all systems constantly evolve, and be totally correct.
As it says on the cover of another of my books,
"Everything is exactly as it should BE, else it would BE different".
So, you can let go of all the "...If only..." (excuses), because they are all nonsense. Ultimately.
The systems best able to adapt to their immediate environment, achieve the best chances of continued life; from the perspective of beast only?
Brain over brawn!
To adapt is to survive and if we survive we can evolve.
We always evolve.
Some may consider obesity as a man-made curse.

One could say it is based around a paradigm completely devoid of love, though in truth, there is much service to self here by many, so not completely devoid of love then.
People get fat through choice and availability of fat inducing foods consumed out of proportion with the health or true needs of the body in mind.
There is a breakdown in the process of fat metabolization within our own bodies.
This breakdown is caused due to eating foods made with refined white flour and/or sugar;
along with refined carbohydrates and chemicals usually.
If we STOP eating foods made with white flour and/or sugar, or foods that are too high in refined carbohydrates, insulin levels in the body returns to normal, over time and health, returns to the system.
Glutens out too!

Some doctors in the western world are threatened if they advise the public of the truth regarding health and sustaining the system we call the body, to extend life as we perceive it.
Fear, poor personal integrity and weak personal values, cause some 'health professionals' to contribute to your death.
That's right. Some doctors, and others, can knowingly be a party to your death.
That in and of itself, is most unloving.
Is this how we accumulate what we identify as 'sin'?
By knowingly doing something that will harm another?
It sounds suspiciously like murder to me.
Or manslaughter perhaps?
And here it is wise to remember, 'a thought is as good as a deed'.
Why is this said?
Again, remember where the real and true power lies.
It is within ourselves.

As we think and speak,
we see.
We hear.
We touch
We smell.
We taste.
We create what we speak in mind!

.
...
......
....

abracadabra

And so,
we can see the importance of loving thoughts, of seeing the good in all things, through understanding and balance.
When parents are devoid of patience, will their children be the same?
When parents are insulin resistant, will their babies be the same?
Is the pancreas flooding insulin into a system that is now insulin resistant?
Due to unnaturally high levels of sugars and refined carbs that the body cannot process.
So, it stores the energy as fat. Along with the toxins.
What of Doctors?
This vicious circle.
It is nurtured and endorsed by some doctors and government puppets and health company puppets.
Doctors are afraid to tell you the truth and save your life perhaps?
It is known that they get HUGE financial incentives, to be a

complicit party in your own or your children's death; think cancer!

What of governments?

Most all governments are run by puppets dancing to the tunes of paymasters.

If puppets don't perform, they are removed;

By death, if necessary.

They are controlled by businessmen.

Companies and corporations controlled by a few, driven by their own egos and greed.

How refreshing it would be, to feel free and trusting towards oneself and the world.

How refreshing it would be, to feel like you could really trust a 'politician'.

How revolutionary would it be, how empowering, to remove the need for governments altogether perhaps? Now there's a thought (changetheworldnow.org?).

Companies are the toys of a few.

Others buy into a dream and we see growth.

Buying into the dream is how others get rewards. It's how they secure their own survival.

Sometimes they feel like they belong. Through that sense of security in that survival. While it lasts.

The single bond is greed and money.

Each paints a picture that holds nothing of value in this world.

All is simply individuals in control (the need for control itself is a state of mind in error).

All are invested in fear and greed.

They are devoid of love towards others, saving it for themselves, and prepare for their suffering perhaps?

Certainly, delays in expanding awareness are apparent. There is much balancing to be achieved.

Could one define weakness by attachment?

Which is fear of loss or going without.

As we believe we deceive and manipulate others, so, we invest in self-deception.

Ensuring our own survival and little else, though obviously temporary.

All things happen through freewill.

Free will is the greatest gift we have.

Because we choose. It is all on us, as it were.

We can hold onto a belief. We can invest in faith.

Faith has its own rewards.

Having faith in oneself to do the right thing. To say the right thing. To be the giver and receiver of love. To lead by example. To treat all perfectly because that's how you expect all other-self to feel and act towards you and again all other self.

Everything we are is in our mind, in our awareness. All we perceive in this world, we discover through our senses.

We can, see with love. We can touch with love. We can hear with love. We can smell with love.

We can even taste with love. Ultimately, we can do everything, with love in our minds.

To see with love is to look with beauty in mind, and compassion.

To view from a position of humility. With a sense of knowing the nature of that which is full of beauty to you.

Humility reminds us of our origin. Of what we truly are; of how we sit in the scheme of things and the biggest picture of all.

When we begin here as a baby we are all the same. We all start at the beginning.

This is the same way we create artificial intelligence.

What we put in, we know will come out.

Think about that!

Children that are shouted at learn to shout.

Children that are belittled become timid.

Children that see or receive violence become violent or

become a victim.

Children can see all too much of this at home, only to have it reinforced in different ways at schools from those in charge, to peers. It's a dog fight unfortunately, in many instances.

Belittling and weighing down young impressionable minds with guilt!

Ultimately, homes and schools are a breeding ground for error. Children need family, they need loving kindness. Children need all family.

This is where we learn, by example as observed.

In the loving arms of family perhaps?

Safe and secure. Where no stresses to survive are evident.

Where community is strong and supportive to all it serves as a whole.

We each teach our children our most modern communication tools.

A language - common to all.

A second language perhaps?

Reading and writing skills.

The world of things recorded.

Different media for exploration, if required and available.

Growing up, playing, having fun and being creative.

All in an environment of unconditional love. No anxieties and no fears.

Our children, all children, regardless of anything at all, deserve, and have a right to grow up in a Garden of Eden.

We can relieve any and all pressures on all families.

So, the support is there from community, for community.

Again, without judgement.

To be of service, without resentment.

Without thought of reward, unconditional service to all.

Just to ease the imbalance in anothers awareness, is to radiate love, and help them find the space to discover love of their own, which they can then share on, and so on.

This always helps us to find balance and self-control in one's self.
Money is an enslaving device. A method for control.
It serves no other purpose but that.
We can barter.
People do barter.
But that is essentially just the same. Because all forms of transaction, hold within themselves the seeds of dissatisfaction and resentment as potential.
The seeds of greed and avarice.
Of lust and wanton desire.
On the other hand, giving as needed can be a selfless act. It is one that empowers self and other self. Simple gratitude and humility on both sides works well. To give in to humility, is to understand the abundance of mother nature's gifts of love to all life. To receive in humility is to be in awe of the power and wisdom of mother nature, due to the nature of our shell and its harmony of existence within the arms of mother nature.
We consume with gratitude, for the sacrifice of foods to service the continuance of life here.
The gifts of mother nature's love holds within, the seed of unconditional love and empathy. A perfect example of giving, unconditionally.
What can we give?
Anything.
Everything.
Retaining love of self to balance.
Where there is true need, let us all provide. Where there is despair, we can offer hope. Solutions - free of any cost.
We can do this little by little.
A thing here, a thing there.
An hour here, an hour there.
If we have no need for something, someone else may need it.
So, we could give it to them, and be enriched and fuelled by

the joy and happiness on the recipient's face.
Payment enough for sure.
This is happening now.
You can join in too, by exercising your freewill.
Why would you do this?
Because we are changing the world
right now, as you read these very words.
Deep inside,
your love is desperate to be free.
To radiate to all who need it.
To freely give in some way.
To contribute freely, knowing it will make the right difference in the world. Then, **not to** seek favour for what you do.
Or you will end up *doing*, just to *receive.* As billioaires do.
Developing expectations like, "I deserve a Nobel prize", or something silly like that. A nonsese, and recogised as such!
All over the world like-minded people are grouping together now.
Because we are all seekers at heart.
We all know when something is wrong or not quite right.
We know a morally or ethically bad situation.
We feel it in our guts.
That's our solar plexus, linked to our soul, guiding us towards truth.
If only we could find the courage within ourselves, to always do the right thing. The world would be so different.
Because It takes REAL courage to look at ourselves, and be ready to receive criticism from self and others, that we embrace and act on, to change ourselves and our lives for the better.
We ALL have that choice.
As we change, we expand our awareness.

The parent that threatens a little child might do well to pause

and reflect back to when they were a child.
What was good enough for you then, may not be seen as good enough now, by you for your children.
Now you can begin to embrace an expanding awareness.
Or maybe to view some adults drunk. Thoughtless. Unloving and blind to truth.
Does it really take a man or woman to hit and punish a helpless little child, to set things right in a situation?

Violence identifies a total lack of self-control,
as well as the feeling of zero control of the situation.
We feel fear when feeling out of control,
so, we totally suppress and dominate,
through anger and violence, as necessary
towards the innocent and helpless,
when it is all in our minds!

How does an adult feel?
When subjected to uncontrollable violence?
Pissing their pants, scared?
So, how would a child feel, when a full-grown adult, towering over them,
beats down on their helpless little bodies, often uncontrollably?
There is no love for a child in a violent home.

Find the love within yourself - End the violence. Now!

Love of self and love of others. A powerful combination.
How many people in the world comply with something, anything, out of fear?
Fear of losing something.
Losing …
your job?

your house?
your car?
your money?
Or
Losing ...
your life?
your mind?
your partner?
your children?
your family?
your integrity?
your own self-love?
Words are great.
But physical action brings about change.
And without change,
there can be no progress.
We must deviate from the norm.
Then we can realise change and growth. New is different. New is growth.

~*~

To wake well rested.
To view the prospects for the coming day with awe, wonder and excitement.
How great is that?
To wake, and know that all is well in your world.
That all are safe
(including you).
That all are fed.
That all are housed.
That all have freedom and security through that freedom.
We all contribute to the whole through loving deeds.
As we think loving thoughts.

By interacting in a loving and compassionate way.
We can begin to view this planet our home as what it is. A place that is to be cared for.
Cared for with an empathetic and loving hand. A hand in balance with heart and mind.
For here lies the future for our children.
Infinite generations.
Infinite love and growth.
The future is ours to create.
We are on the cusp of everything, always.
To consider our evolution is over, that we have reached a level the likes of which cannot be bettered in some way, seems an about face on the working of creation perhaps?
So, it isn't going to happen. Because we are immortal in our awareness.
Now, we wake up to the fact that the human race can die out as a species, but this home of ours will continue to be.
And at some time in the future, will again provide a platform to support the awareness, as we journey in expanding that same awareness, together as ONE.

~*~

I am mindful here of the notion of 3rd and 4th density parallel. As one door closes another one opens.
I have experienced the intertwining of the two and wonder where this awareness sits.
What fun this is.
Consider then, two of you. One to progress on, to experience all done, finding balance and understanding. Another could of course work towards much greater expansion in awareness and embrace the potential of a new age of discovery and unity in society. "Change the world now?" Do we create with a view to tomorrow always in the now? Of course.

The options are now seen to be more more interesting.

~*~

It reminds us of the need for harmony.
Harmony in all things.
How strange it is that so much interest could be placed on such things.
Like magic and super powers, on the *outside*. Yet little thought seems to be given to the ultimate power. That found on the insdie!
Or the fact that we all have access to it all.
By taking time to reflect internally.
By beginning to play internally.
As we begin to awaken to that which is present.
To hear, feel and know.
Our image, soul (?), created as is god.
(Our creator by default).
We can refer to this as subconscious. It's just a label after all.
The inner self. ***Awareness*** as I prefer.
We can talk directly to it.
We can interact with it.
We can begin to feel its presence daily in the now.
As we think, we are guided, in the background.
This is how we create. How we think and see.
How we smell, touch and taste. How we hear.
Such is the wonder of 'coincidence'.
If only we but realised the origins of all the things in our life.
All that we are aware of.
We, are the only shoppers. No one pushes our trolley but us.
We sow, we reap.
The simplicity in all things is simply amazing.
If you harm, you harm yourself.
If you love, you feel love all around.

And if you remove yourself from unloving environments, which is an amazing act of self-love because it can heal or strengthen all involved, through the change itself.

If you are not feeling love in your life, you are in the wrong place perhaps?

You need to change location or perhaps the people or things around you.

Maybe everything.

No sacrifice is too great, in following the ONE path.

If you act as you would like others to act, then like will attract like.

Plus, you can inspire others.

You can help them find the courage within themselves, to be loving and compassionate.

To find humility.

To find the love within yourself is to see love in all life, and in all things in awareness.

With love comes strength. The strength to build faith.

To have faith is to have courage.

The courage to act and make changes.

Changes within and without your awareness.

This is stepping onto the path to ONE.

Never act in any way that will harm others. Sitting down discussing toxicity is hard. Though never someting to be forced onto another self. Never something, to be forced upon anyone at all.

A tough challenge, but one filled with reward for all concerned, if approached with love and truth in mind.

Nurturing an environment of trust within the home takes work and dedication. Where all feel free to lovingly identify error, with a view to progress and growth. To speak out in love for self and other self. If no one tells you of error, you may never see it!

So that those who find error within themselves, have the

courage to see the truth, and to understannd the critique is for the benefit of all.
The necessity for change, sits within all of us alwaysuntil we reach harmony with the ONE.
And so, things do change, and they grow in love.

To err is human.
To forgive is divine.
Simplicity.
To live without need, is to live in comfort.
The human bean is a wondrous creation.
So much so, that we are still in awe of our own, intricate complexity.
Frustrated to some extents by its hidden secrets.
The true subtleties of our physical body and its inner workings may be beyond our appreciation for some time to come.
Of course, the greatest place for the human bean to explore, is the world of inner self.
Here we can discover the voice of our true nature.
It is here, through an attention to consistency in effort and belief, through a developing intention and expectation, that we can discover much more. BEcome, so much more. See the change with expectaion of self, with intent.
It is the greatest realm to discover.
It is a realm of peace and tranquillity.
A place we can explore and create in.
A place we can become aware of and its effects on our 'conscious' world.
The conscious world, the place where we experience through our five senses.
Here we grow.
For as we believe, So, shall it be.
That is with the inner and outer world.
Understand your freedom to create.

.
...
......
....

abracadabra

So much is said of meditation.
So much is said of love.
So much is said in hatred.
So much is said in ignorance, blind to the truth that sits within us.
To hear a voice of wisdom shouldn't we be silent?
For the most distant, quiet voice,
carries the most rewarding message.
The greater the search within, the greater the yearning for truth, the more we can grow and do grow. The more we find through intention and expectation
We deliver unto ourselves, all that which we desire, after all!

Love should never hold fear or regret within its meaning or experience.

Love is not sex.
Yet love is energy in motion.
Sex holds within its experience, the potential for the transfer of energies.
To bring balance to those that would commit to the notion of the passions that can arise, as an experience of love making.
Of divine creative forces intertwined. The energies receieved.
The service.
We feel driven to do and say, to give and share.

Love pours forth through compassion and empathy as we create peace and harmony.

The greatest love is not tied.

It is free to be.

To grow.

It simply is.

Sex of the beast is both for purpose and to also feed a need. The need, is a need for unity, which is never found in the lower self, or the lower acts of the beast that acts without a notion of love or of the energy divine in potential as a part of the physical union.

The actions of a BEast come from an urge of a base nature. One that is self-serving. Basic procreation to service the ongoing needs of the species, nothing else. One that holds no true promise for the sharing of energies in the moment.

Love on the other hand, is Infinite, Unconditional, Natural and Divine.

Yet natural is also born of our senses.

For here is our anchor to this experience, cemented by the veil of confusion.

It is inherent of our physical being to nurture life.

Divine love is of a nature, born of the infinite.

The infinite is beyond our current awareness and yet it just is, and always will be.

I feel a drawing towards the infinite.

To stand side by side with myself perhaps.

I feel compelled to suggest that our species' present course of actions is one of self-destruction.

Though the control lies elsewhere, a lack of self-determination in the whole (humanity), provides an easy road for those who wish to run it with control in mind.

A road of, one might say, evil.

Yet evil is just a word, another label to help identify in

common, a perception of action and other things,
Yet here it is. To deceive all human beans.
To chase money over people's lives;
through food, and through medicine perhaps?
All Beans associated with these, and other dismissive actions,
through an unawareness of their loveless outlook perhaps, still
prepare for themselves a hell, one could say. For payback is
swift.
How else can you begin to find an understanding, and eventually, balance, to allow progression, which is our purpose.
To progress. Besides, the *density of wisdom* will balance all
things. Because *you* CANNOT progress until *you* resonate
at the higher frequency, and can simply merge without the
conflict of different vibrational frequency.
The notion of the Hells is not a pleasant one. I feel for them in
love.
I would implore them to see their error.
To begin to change their world individually.
To save themselves from the waste of repetition.

For there is only ONE path towards growth.
There is only one feeling to grow inside of your awareness.
There is only one notion of purity to ensure you go forward
and not loop in a cycle of self-deception and self-service!
Here and now then, we can begin to see how the meek will truly inherit the earth.
How, through an acceptance and a forgiveness delivered in
mind, those that would subjugate and control, punish and deceive, abuse and dismiss, you WILL grow in the love divine.
Something dismissed or ignored in ignorance by those that are
simply fooled by their own egos born of the beast, the animal
that supports this experience for us all!
To those meek and loving BEings who, while they may not
understand the true nature and/or impact of their actions,

nonetheless, expand their own awareness such that they may not return to the loop of growth in this density of experience. If we commit to change, to change our self, to serve our own growth as we serve the needs of others,
then slowly,
one by one,
we can dismantle the suffering.
Then simply share the glory of the love divine that fuels our very existence.
It is always possible to change outcomes. It is simply a question of Will, like everything.
Beware your own falsehoods.
The potential for the deception of self, fuelled by ego, hell bent on survival at all costs is huge.
Ultimately to slip deeper into the same deception as created by self.
Know your own truths. Know your own error in relation to the ONE path.
We can all begin to see the bean in the mirror with total clarity.
Then we can see the error and make the necessary changes by choice.
All because we can.
Forgetting all the notions and labels associated with behaviour and history.
The reasons for this and for that.
The excuses offered to ease your feelings of guilt and bolster your feelings of self-worth. Re-imagining, re-engineering the emotional record is good to make change?
All the nonsense found in the whisper of the deluded.
The nonsense that seeks to find reason through engaging the intellect, of the all-powerful Human BEan.
The god like creature of ego and self-importance, that trades truth for bombastic self-indulgence, based on the ignorance

and blindness of others.
The meek and mild perhaps?
Base your new experience on nothing more than desire, from a yearning so strong, it creates that which you desire, because you simply can!
Success here, can be found in the depth of your intention and expectation alone! *See the changes within, create your truth, engage with e-motion!*
Feel the growth within.
Feed the love.
Open the eyes wider still,
and live in the present, to change as needed.

To accept truth from others without question; for we all have a right to our unique perspectives. Billions of unique and valid truths.
It also suggests humility, in the acceptance of the unique nature of every individual.
Understand, you are looking at the individual expressions of the big g, in all other selves as well as yourself.

To grow in self-love removes all vulnerability.
To grow in truth, is to set you free!
SUCH IS THE WONDER OF TRUTH.
To judge is to deflect away from yourself, be wise to this.
And protect yourself from the judgement and projection of others.
To project is an error. It is akin to control.
Towards domination maybe, through the subversion of the mind of another perhaps? It is, to restrict the freedom of another.
To judge openly is to mock.
To judge and mock a child, is to choke the very vitality in their life, their freedom in expression.

It crushes their will.
Such is the potential damage metered out through the notion of "Education" by others. The same can be found in the home, sadly.
When unloving,
we display a mean spirit;
spiteful and childlike.
This child pretends to be an adult.
How many adults spend all their time acting like children?
Or could we simply ask;
How often do we pursue unloving goals?
From any age and perspective.
BEing childlike is not an issue in and of itself.
It can be a mechanism of breaking chains in many ways.
Through the fearlessness of innocence.
Just BE mindful of your own behaviour and motivations.
Thought, word and deed.
Young children, just need love and attention.
We give this over time,
with endless patience and tolerance.
We give them wholesome, unconditional affection when requested.
We remind and reassure them they are loved.
We are there to guide them and provide comfort when needed.
To be good role models for them, as best we can.
To hold our values high as a demonstration of what our values are.
We live our values, demonstrating our values and beliefs as we go through this awareness.
To consciously stay present in the here and now. To BE real!
To be open to change and growth in all things, by all things.
For we know this is the way of creation and existence.
We know that change is ever present and affects everything in creation regardless of location.

There is no exception to this, not even the big g, god, the creator.
The ONE that is all things in our awareness.
For the change that is ever present represents the growth in awareness of the ONE; through the changing awareness of self, as expressed in all that the ONE creates. Like all other self, as perceived.
Through a nature that is infinite.

We radiate love to our children.
An unconditional love born of the awareness of the Divine within self, that is the ONE.
This love is in the warmth we display to all things, to all life in awareness.
We display humanity born of awareness of ourselves here.
Born of the awareness found in the means to experience, as derived by the logos that creates this experience, as the continuation of the infinite and continuous change of the ONE, experiencing self, of which we are a part.
Walk in your own truth.
Build firm foundations for your truth to grow upon.
Be responsible for all you do.
Do not judge, rather accept the freewill of all to simply BE.
To BE themselves as they so desire.
Be open to honest feedback if you're in error.
I myself am not perfect. The big g is perfect.
I aspire to BEcome the perfection that is the big g.
That is, the deepest longing in my heart's desire.
I will achieve that perfection, when I resonate to join all that is.
Best to become aware of things unseen in self, to allow for the exploration of the notion of change and growth both without and within.
Do not seek revenge in anything.

For revenge is simply an anchor.
To lock you into a cycle of despair, frustration, anger and hatred. Projected out, yet destroying your progress within.
Rather, find forgiveness through understanding.
With insight and a measure of compassion and empathy to provide the necessary balance which will lead you towards hard found wisdom.
Be tolerant of others.
Be aware of unloving behaviour expressed by you and received by you.
Guard yourself against its influence and the potential to create a cycle of negativity within.
Avoid the mob mentality; be true to self alone. That takes both courage and strength. To BE loving is to understand, you can because you know.
Measure your reason against the truth in your awareness balanced by your heart.

When you have nothing,
and believe you have it all,
the chains of enslavement
will be forever broken.
You will have found the truth in experience of fearless freedom.

Understand the relevance of mother in "mother earth".

Be grateful for all the sacrifices made, to bring sustenance to this vehicle she provides, to carry you during your time in this experience of awareness.
Such is her grace and love for you.
Express your gratitude with every mouthful of all she provides and ALL those that provide it.
That would be, for example, the very plants.

That sacrifice themselves so you may continue to live in the glory of the truth in experience, that is the infinite and ongoing expression of the ONE true creator.

Be wise to cause and effect.

See any damage you cause and own it. In this way you will grow.

Respond with passion. Repent and forgive.

We begin to change, now.

Hold steadfast,

with your moral and ethical beliefs.

Wear your values daily,

as a shield to error.

Be aware to error but don't judge.

Don't condemn or punish.

Allow reflection, and personal space to grow through change in all things.

To focus in truth on what we see in the mirror.

To accept what we may truly appear to be.

Then see with clarity and empathy, the error within, and embrace the opportunity to change through exercising self-control.

Offer unconditional love to all, including yourself.

Respect all life, including your own, for all life is precious.

All life has meaning. All life has purpose.

All life experiences constant change, both within itself and in its surroundings.

Growth through change is the purpose of life as it constantly changes awareness.

Reflect on the care we must give the planet.

How grateful we should be to exist within such biodiversity.

Such unparalleled magnificence… save for our own awareness of course.

The truth here, is that we are a part of this biodiversity.

We need to become aware and understand how all this is

made for us.
So that we can exist here and grow.
So that we could be grateful for its existence.
Perhaps, we may even begin to be careful to conserve life.
Because we have developed a greater understanding of how precious it all is.
In all the things we do, if we simply correct error;
with this notion of constant change as our new paradigm, things will change.
And Life will become better.
When we are given shelter, with freedom and independence and an opportunity to become master of our own world, we grow a sense of appreciation and gratitude for all we have.
Then we can begin contributing to the community as a whole.
Bringing reward to the community and self-esteem to ourselves.
And so, we begin to love life and enjoy relaxed contemplation, as we reflect on the gifts of existence here and now.
With daily reflections we move forward in creativity, with growth towards refinement of our thoughts, aspirations, hopes and dreams.
We enjoy our time in awareness and the lifestyle improvements we now realise.
There are reductions in stress in a general sense, which become widespread as we share and enjoy all these things.
Here then, we begin to understand that it is the changes in self, amongst any and all individuals, that will all contribute to the changes in social thought and social energy as a whole.
We begin to see a change as the paradigm shifts and develops towards one of understanding and the need for gratitude as we experience all that is as a growing awareness.
That being true with ourselves, allows for the development of self in new and glorious ways.
For when there is reduced stress and life is easy for all of us,

which is so easily attainable, then contentment and gratitude in simple pleasures grow in the minds of humankind.

In this new-found space that we now enjoy, we breathe a different breath.

We consider the actions of us as 'adults', yet we constantly grow in recognition of the child within, the player on the stage of life that we experience here and now in the present.

As children, we won't play if we're not loved, especially by our self.

We may sulk, trapped in a cycle of confusion.

We may get spiteful, fuelling our anger with deflections and feelings of lack.

We may blame everyone else except ourselves, as we miss the signals of truth showing our sadness.

We deflect, we hit, we scold, we abuse, we judge.

We're afraid of many things.

We get angry when we lose control or don't understand.

We can hang on to the past, trapped in the cycle of despair and sadness.

All these things limit our ability to be present, in the present. We can find the truth through internal reflection. Through an honest approach to error, with acceptance and forgiveness as our main tools to dissipate the negativity.

Breaking free of the cycles of sadness, anger and despair, through forgiveness based on a growth in understanding of the way of all things.

But what of the present?

Disharmony in a general sense perhaps?

What is the current paradigm?

One of curtailing freedom with a view to manipulation of the masses to serve the whims and wishes of a very small minority perhaps?

What are the current belief systems?

That happiness is obtained through the acquisition of some

thing called money. When in reality of course, it is no *thing* at all. For it is simply a notion.

How is there purpose in what we do here and now?
Because through our experience, we expand our awareness.

What is the purpose of what we do?
To expand our awareness through experience, increasing our knowing.

Benefit is found in the greater understanding of the power of Love as the creative force in the universe. We have previously talked of the meaning of life and the reasons for being here. The more we consider new things, the greater its influence on our considerations.
We avoid panic in our awareness by believing that we know. Whether we actually know the truth of something is, to all intents and purposes, neither here nor there.
This is because we have shifted our awareness to a mode of calm acceptance. We can simply think "oh, ok. That's the way it is".
Should we find something different at a later moment in awareness, we can simply say "Oh, that's the way it is then". And appreciate the… update.
Labouring on error is to be trapped in error. For no other purpose than to experience the negativity, which is a pointless exercise *when you consider our reason for being here. Which is to expand our awareness of the power of love.*
Nothing more and nothing less. Simple.
The notion of punishment when someone makes a mistake, serves no other purpose than to exercise a perceived need for revenge for the action taken.
The suggestion of "an eye for an eye" is simple error.
It harbours within itself all manner of negative energies that

serve only to move awareness in self away from the notions of love that creates all that is.

Consequently, we change our direction away from moving towards the ONE that is all things apparent in our awareness.

How could things change, to foster a dramatic change in thought amongst the whole (as in human beans), to realise the most dramatic and meaningful transformation humankind has ever witnessed or been a party to?

Here, one could be forgiven for momentarily forming a link between a major change and the phrase evolutionary step.

When we deviate from what is considered the norm or current, progress is possible.

Because without change there is no progress!

We could pause here and ponder how quickly we could move forward as a whole?

How would things change in *a world of human beans unified in a single cause*?

Wow, such a notion.

This would be progress like never seen before. Cooperation between all peoples towards a common goal on an unprecedented scale. The common goals being food and shelter, equality and security for everyone regardless of anything. That way, everyone is looked after and more likely to BE happy and content. Giving to community as community gives back.

For change to be implemented with truth and love by all, we must all be on the same page.

We must share a common goal, common values, common passions, desires; we must feel engaged,

Aware of a sense of purpose for the greater good that ultimately benefits all.

Knowing in our hearts that this is safe; the best option, the only option with loving intent.

How could we move forward individually and collectively?

To ensure we give ourselves the best chance of collective progress?
We could embrace the notion of truth, and all it entails. We could build faith based on intuition and some reasoning.
Finding solutions in simplicity. In harmony with mother nature.

The only lasting foundations are built in the minds of individuals, which are shared and embraced to all, around. So that in a short space of time, people change. They change their expectations of self and other self. They understand and reinforce the notion of space, learning, correcting self, and BEing the best, we can. As individuals.
The importance of being present, not living in the past, or dreaming of creation without action.
BE present,
our thoughts can trail off.
Our imagination can kick in, then we have lost reality and find ourselves wrapped up in an emotional storm, as we imagine the worst and live the fears and angers of our waking dreams.
We must greet the day with an intention of calm presence, for it is just another day; full of opportunity to witness the wonders of creation. Our creation.
The bliss in Nature, in every turn and point of reference.
At all points of interaction, we can pause and listen to our higher self.

To listen is a loving act.
It suggests an importance of that witnessed, which is knowing.
As such, we give time/awareness where we can.
Which is what all children seek. Attention, where we find service to others rewarding.
Determine what the speaker wants perhaps?

Is it just attention, or comment or advice or opinion?
Does it matter?

From a position of unconditional love, we can face anything.
From this position we can also determine truth at each moment based on nothing more than intuition towards love.
What our values could be. What they could BEcome.
What aligns with our values? What doesn't align with our values, what needs to change or be removed from our awareness.
Personally, I am always attracted to simplicity.
If it's easy, its most likely to get done.
What do i feel?
If we forget,
we find coincidence.
Else, we continue to create;
sowing and tending seeds,
and the universe. Through all the beans.

Will delivers unto you, exactly that which you create.

As you believe, so shall it be (because it's your awareness).

.
...
......
....

abracadabra

So, values wise, we have love and god as primary catalysts.
What could come next?
Our home? Yes.

Because it is not ours to destroy.
We must do all we can to maintain our home, this planet, MOTHER earth.
There are no second choices if we poison our home.
Think of our children.
Our children's children; and 1000 generations unborn.
They all need us to mature as human beans.
We could become truly responsible for our actions in our minds whereby, we address concerns over maintaining the integrity of the planet, to ensure we work with the planet. To develop our understanding of the planet and how it will work with us!
To correct errors and make good the damage done. To begin to build with love and in harmony with our surrounding perhaps?
To make it all pristine again!
For then, we have an Eden,
a garden of wonder;
of love, of light and life expressed.
An incomprehensibly intertwined series of dependences.
All of which continues to develop and evolve.
Mindful we are simply a part of the whole process. An integral part. Creators.
Slowly but surely, we become mature human beings. In control of the tamed BEast. The undeveloped ego safely understood and accommodated. Free to BE, but not to project, just BE happy.
In the highest corridors of power where the same drug, a notion of self-importance deludes those on high, with misplaced feelings of superiority. Tis sad they furnish their spiritual home with such nonsense and self-suffering.
Everything begins with the individual.
Let him who is without sin cast the first stone.
Unloving acts carry a self-imposed toll. This is the simplistic

truth of god's system.
Because…
it's all about YOU. It's always been about you.
We must be mindful by being in the present.
We must find love in all things.
Another one of our values?
love god
love our home, earth
love ourselves
love all life
love others
all unconditionally. It is the only way.
'once I love all and all love me,
Together we live in harmony'

We can see the children play.
In every business.
In every government.
Almost everywhere we look.
Our leaders display such profound immaturity and fear.
The biggest fools are those that fool themselves.
The biggest lies are told to oneself.
The first and biggest injustice, we do to ourselves.
We lose love, love of life.
The wonder in the majesty that is all creation.
We create.
Some creations are good, some seem unloving.
Man's actions?
we love
we envy
we judge
we covet
we steal
we bully

we punish
we kill, starve, maim
we poison
we cheat
we destroy
we ruin
we wallow in self pity
we feel guilty, ashamed
out of control, mystified
We seek revenge
We eat for the sake of it
while others starve.
We detach ourselves from awkwardness.
We deflect blame and become numb to truth.
Collectively,
we are a mess.
How can this be so?
How can things be like this?
How can, 1000s of billionaires know that over 18,000 children die through starvation and disease every day, and do nothing? Just overpopulated?
This is perhaps,
the truest indication,
of how small our humanity has shrunk!
With so many human beans dying needlessly each day,
one could say
humanity is dead?
As each of us struggle with the passing moments in a day, we need to pause and reflect. To take stock.
To find our humanity and love again.
I mean real things here. I mean reacting to real feelings.
Feelings that motivate us into action.
Motivating those of us that want to change things.
Some people live in fear of becoming in need, and so we cling

to all we have.
Accumulate all we can to show we have more.
Ah, but life is good (I'm sure).
Though is it?
18,000 children.
I cry sometimes at just the thought of it.
I cannot believe that this is all we are, all we will ever be.
Then I think back to the goal. The experiment.
It makes me wonder of the extremes possible in the minds of the beast.
It makes me wonder what else is to come.
Nothing surprises me where the nature of BEast is concerned.
1,000 billionaires. They get together.
They can change the world with loving intent, to bring back Eden?
No, just more control. But we can change all things.
So there is no more fear and no more need.
So that there is hope every day. A light at the end of the tunnel? Or, just no more tunnels?
And we are content.
If we stay as we are, stay where we are and prosper?
Can we share our prosperity?
With all?
All here? Of course.
And all who come to visit, wherever that may be.
Indeed, when we all *have*, life will be good.
When we all have, and there is no need. What then?
When there is no need for laws as we all self-regulate! OMG!
When love is the very fabric of our existence, when it consumes us, what then?
Will we be on the path to Eden? No. We will be in Eden.
The wonder of creation is such that we have all we need here.
This has always been the case. If it was wanted.
When we stop focussing on fear of survival and simply share

all we have with a view to sustaining all life, things will be good for everyone.

The supplies of things are limitless so we can manage with love and share for the benefit of all?

All so easy.

Amazing that no one has thought of this before. Or have we?

We can freely share.

We can nurture life. All life.

The single thing we have to do is take it, this notion of freedom for all, as ours.

Demand it.

BEcome it.

See it, feel it, hear it, taste it, touch it.

The wonder is at our feet.

Not before us.

Not behind us.

We simply choose to pick it up,

Now!

Can you find the courage inside to be different?

To be real?

To be loving in all aspects of your life in your awareness?

This is a big fear in many people.

People get hung up when mistaken with the notion of change.

Of how change from a divine perspective will change them.

It is NEVER a case of "I just want to start singing hymns and walking the streets begging for money or telling people to repent their sins."

Moments of clarity can be quite stark in their 'slap in the face' arrival at times. But in a general sense, people simply change the things they think and the actions they take. *Awareness of truth grows as we take on board new awareness. New awareness leads to new considerations and to new actions.*

This is the true awakening. Yes, we can consider and plan for a resurrection of self, but truly, is your mind/awareness ready for such a step?

Growth in awareness is an ongoing process, as your awareness regarding something specific changes.

The notion of "Enlightenment" as an experience of being at ONE with ONE (our creator), is dependent on your current state of progress, and sits literally thousands of years away with more cycles to go through. The awe so often referenced, is simply the awakening to the truth of our own immortality, as expressions of the awareness of the big g; and the reality that is the awareness of all in progress, as the veil of confusion lifts on passing/dying.

Or, if we become aware of our higher self through inward considerations and explorations.

PAUSE here, and consider this truth in your awareness.

The reason for sharing awareness is to bring new potential into the mind/awareness of other self, to gain a true faith in the creator, to bolster and feed your longing to know of god and feel the love that is divine.

To feel this as an individual, is to become empowered with truth. *The truth is reassuring as we consider our journey here, and all that lies beyond.*

When you see things in a different way, feeling simply like you know something new, something that tells you with a sense of logic and the application of your intelligence that it feels right, because now you *see*. You see within.

This is a process that includes what we can call intuitive awareness. That which comes from the higher self as it were. Suddenly you think, yes, it all seems to piece together nicely. It seems simple, true and free. As it cost me nothing to change direction or realign my desires with truth!

A new confidence in the reassurance of truth in your awareness regarding purpose, time here and the future; and of course, the real nature of the ONE creator.

New awareness can often be a visual experience. To see new

is to create within; creating awareness in truth. Hence the simple visualisations shared at the beginning of this book. Sowing seeds of truth in awareness, to bring a sense of knowing more, and feeling better for it.

As simple as when someone says, "I was at such an' such a place over the weekend."

And because you've been there in mind, you have a knowledge of it. A picture of your last awareness of it may become apparent. Remembering the look and feel of the place.

A smile, as you flood your awareness with more pictures you can associate with. This is knowing. A familiarity brings a sense of ease, as opposed to a dis-ease.

As we visualise anything, we enjoy the notion of something again.

In this way, we can BEcome aware of the notion of our own focus, of our own awareness.

In a moment of still awareness, we consider the darkness, after we close our eyes.

In this space of infinite black, we focus on a single point. A spark. A motion? A repeat of the same. Do we have a vibreation?

Thoughts and images may bombard our awareness, so we let them drift away by a simple acknowledgement and focussing on the still of the dark within.

That movement of matter. The same sensation as when we see with our eyes. It is seen, and recreated at will within.

Here I will remind you, our awareness is beyond all we currently perceive, and all we will perceive after passing.

How and why is this so? Because,

the universe is within the awareness of the big g! Which I said much earlier in the book. Think about that, and about us, for we are the same are we not!

So, **creation took place. That a focus based on a desire, manifested all notion of movement and existence in a**

single time/space. Built for it and it alone, as it vibrates at an infinite rate, to BEcome everything there ever was and ever will BE, as it remains constant in its own *infinite rebirths*.

Constantly exploring the probable as the most improbable and so realised somewhere. Constantly expanding the awareness of ONE, which at some point in the journey of each individual awareness, is fully available as we refine sufficiently to join that which is the ONE.

And it is in this moment, here and now, as you read and embrace the notion of the creation of the universe and our own space/time for this experience in awareness, that you grow in awareness through truth.

This new belief of awareness experienced, begins to change your feeling of attraction. Through an expanding sense of knowing.

This is right, that is wrong, this is here, yes, it's there.

Things just work. Things are accepted. Fuss is dismissed and so much more can get done for the fun of doing it. ***Think on that for while!***

That notion of freewill, tolerance and acceptance. Of understanding more, about the notion of why?

Perhaps I could simply say, "Why anything?", and instantly reply, "Why not?".

Here we can begin to see the reason for some occurrences. For any and all occurrences.

Understanding that everything that can BE, will BE. And by virtue of that alone is everything then, acceptable?

Of course, to someone. Don't forget that experience is experience for all.

And so, it goes on.

It is worth reminding ourselves here of a truth.
If you are aware of suffering and have the means to END the

suffering, but do nothing, it must be a conscious decision.
Where has the good Samaritan gone?
To observe free will does not mean to avoid despair in what you see. Wisdom beckons...
What of compassion?
To feel a need. A need to feel? To BE in need? To BE that which is needed?
To imagineer for the sake of Love and nothing else.
To create change in a loving way or ways.
To BE a positive difference in the life of another self is perhaps the greatest honour and duty available to us here in this awareness.
So, we can 'teach them to fish', we can give them the gift of freedom in any desired education.
Here I mean desired, as in, there exists a passion within themselves to drive them on.
We would be wise to teach them to fish. In whatever way that translates to each particular set of unique requirements and circumstances.
So much could change over a single year.
All we need is love (heard that before).
Love promoting action.
Action observed by others.
Inspiring others to grow in love.
Trust is imperative.
Finding the good in people.
Trusting in their love.
Observing some error, understanding error. There but for the *grace of god* (my own awareness) go I.
Finding compassion and empathy. See above.
Forgive error in behaviour, without judgment. See above.
Self-love keeps us safe from harm, unless we are attracted to it.
To be free, we just decide to be so, and it is so.

We see it as so, and it becomes truth.
Such is our creativity, and experience through action. We co-create our reality in every moment. We must always determine our own path and be free in spirit.
Change is afoot.
Different decisions and choices are being made every moment.
You choose when you can. You accept when you have to perhaps?
This is also evolution of course. The evolution of the individual. Of Society?
That remains the choice of Society. Through self control in the individual. Service to others, or service to self?
Like the masters of food and pharmaceuticals, who craft and secure their very own unique and individual future.
The product it needs to survive; that would be us.
Something to consume the food that does not promote good health.
So, we get sick. Through a lack of self control.
Then there's the cowardly medical empire.
That rubs its hands together with the chemical companies and some food companies.
It's like a vicious circle as between them they breed death.
Mind you, it is a death we embrace so often it seems. Why is that?
Hundreds of millions of suffering, all too blind to change.
So self-consumed, they trudge towards death.
The complicity is key of course.
The dealers of disease and sickness, a master plan.
The complicity of the medical world so often realised.
Discarding their own values, ethics, their morals.
Closing their eyes to the suffering and futility.
The inhumanity of it all seems almost inhuman, yet here it is, in humans!

What happened to all these people? Fear and loss of Free Will.
Fear, greed, weakness?
And while they feather their own nests here, they also feather nests in the afterlife so to speak. Much to experience then.
There is balance to be found in experience!

I feel so much for all these lost people.
I send them all love, that they wake and become real.
And begin to become aware of their future suffering.
As now, the time has come to see the simple truth and change their lives.
No amount of suffering is ever acceptable.
The true weakness of millions of people in positions of power, is the single reason, why, there should be no power at all?
The frail little ego of the human BEast is incapable it seems, of controlling power as perceived, whereby they treat all other self with a sense of equality.
This is a big problem for human beans.
We are changing the world.
Is the world becoming a better place?
If it isn't, it's our error collectively.
Forget blame, make change through action for the benefit of all of us.
Error always paves the way for change (Don't touch that, remember!),
Change can lead to progress (Excellent. Didn't get burnt), or not (ouch!) forgot.
All of god's children can now come together in truth and be free. So simple.
Exercise your right to choose.
BE free.
Change now.
For different tomorrows.

Tomorrow

Tomorrow we woke up, and it was today!

Things would never be the same again;

and all the human beans were happy.

It went like this,

.

...

......

....

abracadabra

Warning. Turning this page could suggest you are a seeker!!!

The Single Revolution, for Evolution
based on the book, "Charlies Poem" by Roy Thomas Dow.
Available from 1331 PRESS (roydow.com)

The lady with the clipboard listened intently; waiting for direction from the production booth.
He could hear the noise of the crowd.
They had been warmed up and then fed, as required, by their 'oh so' professional host, Henry Thornton.
One of the most accomplished chat show hosts of this century!
Bent as a nine-bob note and as camp as you like, but in such a subtle and alluring way. You just want to listen to him speak.
And like the best of the queens, his wit was both sharp and entertaining.
Words just rolled off his tongue. It was as if he could do this in his sleep.
His voice was piped all through the building from the stage.

"... he has given us 'the single revolution for evolution', is he going to change the world, let's find out, Slarty Mcfartbart is here, ladies and gentlemen!"
The lady with the clipboard smiled at Slarty and motioned him to go on stage.
He smiled back and confidently walked forward into the light.
As soon as he was visible, the cheering increased in volume, the applause grew louder. Clearly, they were pleased to see him.
Henry had a wide smile on his face as Slarty moved in for the shaking of hands.
Henry gestured to the seat. Slarty sat, as did Henry. They exchanged grins. The crowd was so loud!
Henry raised a hand for quiet and like good children, within

several short seconds there was silence.
Slarty had his eyes closed. Henry said nothing. You could hear a pin drop. The silence seemed to go on for ages, yet it was just a few seconds.
Slarty was composing himself.
With a deep breath, Slarty opened his eyes and looked at Henry with a big smile on his face.
"Hello Henry," said Slarty. Henry smiled and looked round at the audience.
"Slarty Mcfartbart - ladies and gentlemen! Isn't it such a pleasure to have him here on our little show!" The crowd showed their appreciation.
Henry grins so widely you wonder if he's out of breath.
He shoots a flashing grin across the face of the studio audience. "Yes indeed." He taps his notes on his free right hand. "Now then..."
Once again, the appreciation of the crowd dies rapidly to a silence.
"It seems we have some fans in tonight!"
Some audience members whooped or whistled in agreement.
Again, there was a pause for silence and Henry adjusted his position to face Slarty,
who was reaching forward to drink from the glass of water on the table just in front of his knees.
Slarty quickly scanned the room as he drank.
The lights were so bright. The cameras and wires everywhere. People standing around.
But this was not his first time on TV. Not the first time with a live studio audience. It had caused a stir since the first readings. Snippets given here and there.

The suggestion that the single biggest cause of pain and suffering has had its day and was about to be removed forever. It was unprecedented.

No one thought it was possible. Almost everyone had had their doubts; but somehow, almost everybody on this planet could see the reality. See the need for change.
Now, it was highly desired; even Demanded!
The promise of a new tomorrow, soon, just a single revolution away even.
"Right, so, we have already met and had a chat in the green room, but I must say, nothing was given away regarding the book. You wouldn't talk about it backstage.". Slarty grunted an acknowledgment as he nodded. Henry continued.
"Which kind of left me feeling a little bit uneasy, I must admit."
Seizing the moment (ever the true professional), he spun his head round towards his close-up camera, pouted his lips slightly, and whispered, not too quietly,
"sort of like a first date really". He was a master of camp theatrics.
His eyes sprang wide open as he swung his head back around with a swish.
Many in the audience tittered, some laughed. Slarty laughed. Henry held the book up to show the camera and audience.
"Here it is ladies and gentleman, "Charlies Poem", the little book that's changing the world it seems?"

Henry was a good host and he knew it, which usually made him confident. It was his professionalism that made the spots. He never missed a beat.
"The book has been the most amazing success. So much so that here we are now.
To say it has touched the lives of people is of course an understatement."
Slarty nodded.
"I did find it a very different book; I'm not sure why.
I mean it is quite a confronting book and yet while it caused

controversy, the people have embraced its message wholeheartedly...?"

Henry paused, struggling somewhat.

"Beautifully put Henry," said Slarty knowingly. "if I could cut in..." he gestured with his hand as in rolling along, to continue

"Please do," said Henry, pleasantly surprised and a little relieved.

As Slarty began to speak, Henry bent forward and got a drink of water from the table in front of him. the lights seemed particularly hot today, and a bead of sweat rolled down the side of his head.

Henry received a jog from the production booth,

"make up coming in"

off camera, Henry received swift assistance, beaming all the while.

The camera's zooming in for close ups as Slarty spoke.

"The concept for the book is a simple one, Henry. Its focus is on truth and love. On ensuring all of our tomorrows being the best todays they could ever possibly be.

Removing money as the enslaving device it is, simply because it is the will of the people, nothing less, and what the people want, the people get.

It's a pointer towards the truths of the distant past. Of our heritage.

There is an importance to just BEing aware here.
Learning from previous errors. BEing aware to the simplicity in cycles.
Finding we have faith in our knowledge.
Knowing how things came to BE and where we came from.
Belief is found in awareness. Awareness expands.
It expands to where we believe we can safely venture to.

We are always more at ease within ourselves, until we prefer BEing a part of something bigger.

That something bigger, is the open mind, the expanded awareness, the truth of creation and our place in it.

In the now, we have a greater sense of direction, for experience is in reality as reality is in our experiences; through a sense of presence within the present. This is where your awareness lies.

Always belonging. Otherwise it wouldn't BE.

This is how we grow in love and creativity. We just begin and do. We grow in both love and creativity through boundless expression."

Henry cut in.

"I did notice the book talks about not being judgmental, yet sits in judgement of all of us really. Is that how it should be interpreted?"

Slarty smiled and nodded his head as Henry asked his question. He replied,

"Yes, yes, I can see that.

The main point here, is to understand the need for identifying error, without a need for the projection of judgement onto any individual.

When you name an individual, you affect them personally. Focusing on them.

To hear about collective error is just an opportunity to search within yourself with truth, to correct the error if you need or want to should you find it in yourself."

"So, you're not saying, look what all of you are doing wrong, I'm perfect, do what I say?" asked Henry.

"Not at all," said Slarty calmly. "When I look in the mirror I love what I see. I understand I have much to learn like all of us.

You can say, there is infinite knowledge to learn and always will be. Until we BEcome at ONE with the infinite awareness that is the creator. As awareness, we are always learning, which is always seeking the perfection of truth.

The catalyst that serve us in awareness are meant to help us identify error without apportioning blame because it's not loving to judge and punish in anyway.
It assists those of us that wish to seek true freedom in order to be able to build a better world for all of us.
It is meant to assist us on our evolutionary path.
We are meant to be more than we are and we will be more.
It is a core desire of our father mother god, that is.
Although that in itself falls short of the mark really.
We can simply accept that failure is not a relevant word in a world of unconditional love with limitless creative force.
A world where we create according to desire, and we accept that somewhere, someone will create according to their desire.
The notion of balance in all creation begins to grow in the awareness, and a bigger picture of what the infinite possibility of one, like me or you, or one of an infinite variation of selves, could BE like?
Infinite Reality from Infinite Possibility in Infinite Probability from Infinite Source.
There is no such thing as failure due to the constant change realised within any cycle.
What we agonisingly call failure is nothing more than a realisation, at a specific moment, of the need for change and action to achieve a different result.
This is the truth of our normality that makes up our reality."
Slarty paused and took another drink of water. Henry cut in.
"I must say, Slarty, (love the name by the way)," Henry took a quick, rehearsed swipe to the right for his close-up quip, this time, a face contorted in pain.
"... mummy and daddy hated me..." he pulls a quick sad face as he spins back round to face his guest.
He flashes Slarty a quick, playful grin, then retreats back to his cards. Slarty smiles warmly.
"No, come on..." the crowd giggles.

The two men lock eyes.
"We know, I know, this is very serious stuff. Are you surprised by the sales and the varied reactions around the world?" Henry cocked his head ever so slightly
"Not at all.... abracadabra," Slarty beamed a huge smile towards Henry.
Henry was nodding as he listened, yet a vagueness was apparent as thoughts formed in his head.
"Yes. Now. There's a thing. A lot of people have been talking about the many references or uses of the word abracadabra."
Slarty was nodding as he listened intently.
"People are talking about witchcraft and voodoo and all other sorts of nonsense, so what's that all about?"
Slarty took a deep breath, pausing before answering
"Well Henry, the simple truth is in the meaning of the word. Abracadabra, 'I create what i speak'. It serves as a reminder to be aware of our thoughts. And it also suggests what I'm doing, as in creating."
Again, Slarty beamed at Henry. Having delivered some in depth material and feeling comfortable, he took another big drink of water and relaxed back into his seat.
Henry continued.
'I must say, I never felt there was masses of negativity surrounding the things you say and suggest.
But now, we must talk of the global phenomenon that is the "ONE REVOLUTION - FOR - EVOLUTION" campaign.
Before Henry could even finish the sentence, the audience were beginning to cheer.
"Yes, we all like this... I think?
It really is the most amazing thing. It will... I believe, transform the world in a way that I don't believe anyone would have thought possible, ever."
Henry was very animated at this point. Slarty was happy and all smiles as Henry jumped up from his chair and walked

toward the studio audience.

An assistant rushed towards Henry and handed him a microphone. Henry was going walkabout.

"So, hello, hello, how are you, how are you," he walked amongst the rows and aisles greeting as he went, searching for someone to speak to.

"Oh dear, look at that,"

he paused and stopped at a young man wearing a ripped t-shirt.

"Here we have a fashion statement!" The camera went in for close ups of them both. Henry gently tugged at the shirt and the rips. "Is this a fashion statement or are the ratings so low we fill the seats with the homeless?" Henry pulls a sad face, hangs his head and places a hand on the youth's head, like a papal blessing. With a sigh, a shake of the head, he moves on as the audience, including the young man, enjoys the joke.

He moves to a man who is smartly dressed.

"Ooh, now you sir! You look very well to do. And that's why I've stopped to talk to you. Let's find out what you think about this. We had to find someone with money." Henry paused, to play.

Henry looks back to the man with the ripped t-shirt.

Like mind readers, the production booth pastes the man's face (beaming at the attention), over all the studio monitors.

"Slim pickings tonight it seems." Henry said. The audience erupts.

Henry turns his attention back to the man in the seat next to him.

Henry grabs his hand, inspects his watch, then holds his hand up.

"Dripping with gold and jewellery!"

He points his index finger into the air to signify a pause for thought. the production booth zooms in for a close-up.

"Shit, now he's going to get mugged and they'll say it was all

my fault. Help me ma!"
His eyes rolled as he played with innuendo. The audience roared with laughter. He had them all in the palm of his hand and he knew it.
Henry was in full control and in his element.
"You seem to be quite well to do, makes me wonder why you're here amongst the riff-raff."
Henry looks back again at the man with the ripped shirt, who was still, while laughing heartily, very happy to be the centre of attention periodically.
Again, his face flashes onto the studio screens and the audience responds.
Once more, Henry returns his attention to the man before him.
"Come on then, stand up, let's see you." He stands.
Having stood, Henry once again grabs at the man's arm and looks more closely to inspect the watch.
Again, Henry turns to the camera.
"It's fake," said Henry.
He spun around to the ripped shirt man, "he's not worth it", the audience roared with laughter, then he spun back round to continue with gold man.
"Now then," Henry checks his cards. "quieten down you rabble," he bites.
The audience dutifully quietens down and Henry continues.
"Now, we must be serious for a moment, because fun and games aside, this is perhaps the biggest change in society since... forever. So, you can sit down now fake gold man."
The man sits down.
Henry is grinning at the camera as the audience titters.
"So, have you any fears or misgivings about this new PARADIGM, and, do you think this is a good thing or a bad thing. And do you think it's going to work?"
The man paused, took a breath, then began.
"I've seen other interviews with Slarty and he says we must

take the step if we want to continue the journey, this transformation. I agree with him. It's all about the future for our children.
He said we will all be free. All working together. He said it would be Eden. I believe him."
Henry adjusted his position to talk to the lady in the row behind gold man.
"And you lovely lady. Do you think it's a good thing? Is it going to be the change we all want? To finally bring peace to the world?"
The woman was all smiles and grins, really fidgety. She was quick to reply.
"I would love to see it. I just wonder if people will let us down and it all fails."
Henry turned to a third and fourth audience member, close by.
"And is that the consensus here? Are we all thinking that. Really?" he said nodding, and cast his eyes around to see a sea of nodding heads responding, along with a few verbal confirmations here and there.
Henry turned towards the stage and began to walk back.
"Right then. So that's a few quick thoughts from you lot, now we'll go back and chat some more to our lovely guest, yes."
The audience applauded, like an agreed time fill for Henry's return to his seat.
Once there, Henry addressed the wider audience beyond the camera.
"So, what we have here is the biggest social change in human history. Is it a global event?" He turned to face Slarty.
"Slarty, what are you hoping for? And do you think some people will let us down and it will all go wrong?"
Henry turned and quickly scanned the audience, then zoomed back to lock on expectantly at Slarty.
Slarty was smiling as he listened to Henry, then adjusted his position to speak.

"Well Henry, the biggest areas for concern are whether or not people will play fair. And that is a valid concern. but like all things similar, it is just a fear imagined in your mind. Having faith and leading by example will carry people forward. As Gandhi said, 'BE the change you want to see in the world'. We all want love and to live in peace. So be loving and peaceful.
We all want to BE equal, to treat everyone as equals.
We all want a home with food and a future. The world is big enough, to support us all and always will be.
Fear in the minds of silly Beans, Human Animal Beasts, is what causes the problems. Be fearless.
When we witness goodness and loving intent, we all eventually crumble and break down our own barriers because we can trust and feel as though we belong. We feel a part of everything and then we all help. And because of this helping each other, to make everything easier for all of us, life IS easier for us all, and just continues to get better."
Slarty is smiling at this point, as is Henry. As is everyone, and Slarty continues.
"Economic migration, by reason of poverty, will be a thing of the past. And the power will always sit with the people. Because without us there is nothing. And in this way, the majority will maintain the freedom of all of us."
"Remember Henry, we all want to love and be loved in a wholesome, unconditional way. As brothers and sisters. As one giant family. United in the purpose of preserving our planet, our home, and preserving ourselves.
Being kind and respectful to all life."
Slarty paused. His eyes began to fill.
Henry reached out to touch Slartys arm. "Are you ok?" asked Henry, genuinely concerned.
Slarty smiled as the tears began to roll down his cheek.
'So much love Henry, so much yearning for all this to be

reality. And it is. I can feel it from all these good people." He stood up and addressed the studio audience and the viewers at home.

"It is truly amazing. Just think about it. We, all of us, are truly amazing.

In just 6 days' time, the final R-evolution will begin.

For the majority to agree and decide to travel down this path is deliverance.

This is the road we should be on, because we're on it.

'Cogito Ergo Sum'.

We are creating Eden, right here, right now! We are living this creativity. We are the creation and we are growing. This is progress.

This is what creation is all about, change. Growth.

Expansion in awareness through experience, somewhere.

It's all about love and life, and now it is better. And it just keeps getting better and better. The age of divine love and growth on an unprecedented scale. Welcome to the new age, the Aquarian Age. This, is our moment of evolution!"

The audience erupted in applause and cheers. Many stood. Henry stood and shook Slartys hand as he shouts out to address the audience.

"Yes, come on! This is it people. The one revolution for evolution is coming soon!"

All around the world, hearts were growing in love, and things were good.

.
...
......
....

abracadabra

And so, it came to pass,
that on that day, the anointed day, as the sun rose on the
horizon and passed the zero-degrees longitude at Greenwich,
London, England, the new day began.
A day of revolution through the evolution of millions and
millions of people.
It happened simultaneously, then just kept going.
Seemingly from the top to the bottom; and continued as the
sun chased the surface of our home planet earth. Spinning out
in space. Around our sun.

For twenty-four hours the new start occurred, moment by
moment across the face of the planet.
With total disbelief people woke to the new day and went
about their normal tasks, but there was a spring in their step.
Things were different. Well, in one way they were.
NOBODY, ANYWHERE IN THE WORLD, USED MONEY!!!
That's right, money NEVER changed hands once.
Everyone coped with the fear. It was only momentary after
all.
Once in the groove, it felt fantastic.
Amazing. So weird.
Everyone was smiling. even the retailers who were just giving
stuff away yet nobody took more that they needed to, as guided by all and reminded, they can come back tomorrow if they
need more, like anyone else can.
But it happened. It was true. Money was a thing of the past. It
was no more.
Thankfully, life would never be the same again.
From here on, there was no turning back.
Somehow, everyone seemed to know.
This may be our best, and perhaps, our only chance to get this
right.
Like a one-shot deal.

Which of course it wasn't...
There had been so much speculation in the beginning, when it was first suggested. Even asking if it was true, as in a real possibility.
A course of action for the entire human race.
As in all of us.
It seemed a miracle.
In such a seemingly short space of time,
Word had spread; about a choice that we all had.
And that we all had a voice in this.
It was new. It was different for sure.
Was it something good?
Some were confused for a short while. Many "smart" people just couldn't get it. Just didn't see it!
They were so invested in the system and themselves.
So, invested in the idea of "You can't get something for nothing."
There are none so blind as those that see.
Perhaps, for some, this may well be the case initially.
But with time, they all came around. Such is the power of love.
The truth is, that if we walk into an orchard at the right time of year, isn't there always fruit in abundance for all to eat?
And isn't it free to all who pick it?
Our entire planet, our home, is one of abundance.
It provides for us all, without measure or toll, all we need to LIVE.
To experience BEing.
Now, the starvation and deaths stop. Love is free and growing exponentially.
Moment by moment from that day, that day of wonder, that day of awakening, of revelation, of revolution and evolution. Action and change occurred in a way it never had before and never would again.

There are few things in life as rewarding as watching your children playing.
Knowing that they are safe. Happy and content. Loved and loving. Free to create and Free to simply BE.
This is the day we made our creator's heart soar.
This is a special day, as the collective felt the knowing of the pierced veil of confusion.
At that moment of united expansion in awareness,
Life begins anew.
The notion of creation and the possibilities that grow, are unrestrained, unbounded. On this day, the world awakens to a new collective awareness and exponential growth.

The notion of creating, in the more literal sense, with so much more power to create. It needs to be controlled perhaps? By self, with love in mind.

Reality found in dreams, is created by choice based on free will alone.
it's like... a rebirth.

Imagine, ME

by Roy Thomas
07.06.2021

Imagine waking up one morning,
knowing things just aren't the same
In your mind a distant calling,
hear it calling out your name

Would you then climb back in bed,
through feeling sick, or not, quite right?
Stay on the bridge to see again,
the plan that day and all it might?

What a wondrous day we find,
when we begin to understand
That we create the very spark,
to carry out all things as planned

We seize the moment with our heart
and feel the very stuff of dreams
Emotion filled and action packed,
well that's the way it always seems

A silver platter in our hand,
a motivation coming clear
We see the dream we want to be,
we hear the words we want to hear

Lay the neural pathways down,
cement with purpose everyday

Full of love, desire and hope,
for charity to all we pray

What is, or could, the final dream,
become for all, as once unseen
And so, all walls came tumbling down,
as all the suff'rin' spreads around

Is this the way we all became,
so bashed and bruised from truth in love?
And as we looked around at all,
we all became the single dove

I looked at you, and felt the pain,
no tears of joy, no safe, secure
You looked at me and understood,
the fear and lack of love inside

And so, it was, that we all knew,
how each was made, a single ONE
The empathy that linked us all,
and no one sought to run and hide

The packet mix was all the same,
for all of us in different ways
But now in each, the truth we found,
we understood, without a haze

"Hello ME", I said to each,
and grabbed and shook each hand with love
And then each did the same to ME,
and all the ME's, from up above

We thought about the stuff we thought,
the stuff we said, the stuff we did
The way that life was done by you,
and how you felt, "the other kid"

In every thought and every word,
and every action we BEcame
We felt and heard, well, every word,
and every blow and all the pain

And so, it was, the world undone,
undone by love, we all can see
Accept, forgive and let it go,
and all of us will just BE free

And now we tend each ME as ME,
affording all the love we can
The truth of everything we see,
As ALL, as ONE, we understand

And so, it was, we all began
to pull our heads from out the sand
3 2 1 (click)
… And you're back in the room.

~*~

Conclusion

True power exists in the mind, in our awareness.

Awareness in stillness. It provides a base for growth and understanding, unknown to the beast.
Awareness is THE power! The guiding force. The ultimate. For all comes from awareness of all.
The greatest POWER is that of creation, Love; which is no more than the focus of desire based on intention, formed by your imagination!
"As I believe, so shall it BE" "Abracadabra" (I create what I speak.). It's all about us.

Every Bean, here and now, has the power to create their own reality based on nothing more than desire.
Once the desire is established, things begin to happen based on the power of the focus of the individual.
Ergo, to awaken, to step firmly onto the path of "enlightenment", one simply needs to believe in the process.
That desire, born of self-love, will deliver unto you all that which you desire.
This is the way of things.
This is the way the Universe was created.
It is the way anymore universes would continue to be created, in the infinite dance of creation; as the ONE true creator continues to express and grow, in an infinitely expanding awareness.
Created in the image of the ONE true creator, we are creators. We are not gods, that's just silly. We are not of the same ilk as god, for if we were, we would merge with god, becoming at one with ONE.
Whoever considers themselves more than other self is totally deluded and aware of fantasy, based on the notions of an immature ego, the ego of the human beast, nothing more.
Now, people begin to see ALL the Children in the world! So

many as adults it seems.

To know your place in creation, is to be free of all fear. It is to understand the nature of your own immortality.

Safe in the knowledge of the cycles of growth in which we find ourselves.

This is how we grow to an expanded awareness.

This is how we begin to embrace the notion of "Heaven on Earth".

There is NO Divine Saviour about to come down to earth's surface and save all the sinners, for there are no sinners, as such.

This belief is simply held by all those Beans trapped in cycles of unknowing, or error we could say, as we balance our awareness against the truth of our own existence and the journey in which we find ourselves.

It is a falsehood expounded by religious houses around the world to promote a sense of need, towards those that appoint themselves the voice of all things right and holy.

SUCH UTTER LIES AND RUBBISH. Sown to trick and control, nothing else!

Here is more true awakening.

Here is the knowing.

Here is the faith.

Here, born of now, is the desire for change and growth born of truth in our own individual awareness. Needing NO one else. You don't have to forget all labels, simply remember that they are labels. As such, they identify a notion of something, often at shared times, for common awareness and understanding in communication.

BE mindful of the limits of intellect and reason, and the uses of imagination to assist in the creation of all things new.
Also, BE mindful of the limits of ego as a reasoning tool.
Begin to grasp the notion of awareness as a single state of reference outside of and inside of everything we are aware of.

~*~

The veil of confusion, this LAW of Confusion apparent here and now, is born of a desire to intensify the experience in awareness through the use of catalyst, to promote growth in awareness of truth, born of fear and unknowing.
The extremes of experience here, give way to the revelation of "love conquers all" perhaps?
Even in the more rudimentary animals of this world, we see the devotion of parent to child; with a view towards survival of the child against, sometimes, seemingly impossible odds.
This is the nature of love. To protect that which it creates.
It is one of care and creation. Of continuation in growth and understanding. Of ever-expanding experience and therefore awareness, as new is constantly delivered to the same awareness.
In a perfect world we are all aware.
Yet the perfection falls short in delivering any urgency in growth in awareness, for all who know truth it seems.
Fear is unapparent in this awareness.
The 'sense' of knowing does not promote the desired yearning, one could say. Certainly, this is so when we consider the catalyst of fear, as perceived in the awareness of the unknowing Bean!
"What comes beyond death and how do we know for sure?"
When we embrace this notion as truth, we can begin to understand why we are here, as in purpose.
We are here to grow in the ability to create, based on a desire.

A desire or yearning so powerful so as to become aware of the power of love as a force for creation.

Based on the very same yearning and desire that brings an awareness of the same to self.

Here, we now begin to see and understand why the Law of Confusion exists.

It is such that the creator expands the potential of the experience of self, of which we are!

For in TRUTH, we are ONE.

All is ONE.

When you harm your neighbour, you harm yourself.

When you love your neighbour, you love yourself.

When you help your neighbour, you help yourself.

When you poison this earth, this planet, you poison yourself.

When you love and nurture this planet and all life, you project love and nurturing to all life and this planet, which is here to simply provide the background, the support mechanism for growth in awareness and nothing more; through the experience, born of the catalyst for change.

The catalyst simply nudges us towards awareness and out of the cycles born of the veil of confusion, cast down through this awareness of time passing (space/time).

Here we must simply Believe.

Develop a FAITH.

We can develop trust in the POWER of LOVE, in the DIVINE LOVE.

The force of creation (Will of creator expressing knowing).

The creation of our own knowing, our own awareness.

As we, our self, progress. Refining our own vibration towards a match with that which is infinite.

Which is the big g.

We CANNOT join and become as ONE until we are refined in our own awareness.

Refined as a vibration. To one of an infinite level perhaps?

At that moment, we join all that is. We become a part of the ONE.
For all is vibration, after all.
And so, we progress towards becoming a part of the infinite light of creation.
Then we can transcend to join that which we are born of. That crafted the light of creation through desire.
Here we see the simplicity of the cycle of Divine Creation.

All we lack here is the knowing in our awareness of the truth about our self as creator and all other self as creator.

Therefore, we have no awareness of what lies beyond the veil of confusion, until we do of course.

For then we have an enlightenment. Then we become aware of our own immortality and how we continue on after what we perceive here as "death".

Here, is nothing more than a part of the process of growth towards the infinite.

Begin to grasp *the notion of awareness as the single state of reference outside of and inside of everything we are aware of.*

To grow NOW, we can simply accept the truth as we see it.

"I can see that...". You might say or think within.

Simply believe and it is so.

As such, one then grows with greater speed through embracing truth and losing the notions of the beast, born of those that are unaware and simply seeking to control, based on the notions of their own misguided and unknowing egos!

Silly Beans, eh!

Simply stuck in cycles of what we can call error, without judgement or projection of the same intended, just truth in our own awareness. Shared to act as nothing more than another catalyst for their own awakening to continue!

And so, we begin to become aware of how it all works; and perhaps even a greater understanding of why it is so.

Why it is this way. Because it works.

Of how we are truly a part of an experiment to expand the awareness through experience of self that is the ONE.
That self, being the creator of course.
Of whom we are an expression of, remember!
Born of the same, as the same.
God like definitely, but certainly not a god!
It is just the base ego (that of the human BEast), that sends Beans into cycles of error and nonsense.
Creating catalysts to intensify the experience the other self becomes aware of.
Remember, as we embrace the truth with acceptance we begin to grow.
We begin to lose the fears and cares associated with the unknowing.
Because we simply know truth in our hearts, as it were.
It is that same belief that grows the knowing within.
The knowing that leads us all towards AN EXPANDED AWARENESS OF TRUTH; known here as enlightenment.
Onward Beans.
Find the balance, forgiveness, understanding and love.
In the love and the light of the ONE infinite creator, peace BE with you now!
And so, it is. Shared with Love.
In a moment of pausing,
our mouths become silent and we consider all in our awareness.
We find space; a sense of balance perhaps?
I do think about you all. I do think about all of us. I do think about all of... me.
I am that I am and you are the same.
There is little difference between us in the grand scheme of things.
We share the same journey, all of us. We have the same basic goals, desires, hopes and dreams.

We all create, knowingly or unknowingly.
We all change to become more than we were just moments before.
The simplicity of a single desire is all that's needed to transform your life, your awareness, your BEing, for the benefit of you and all you interact with here in this game of BEing.
To understand the nature of greed and envy is to BE aware, thus enabling balance in desire based on truth in need.
We can simply BE aware to the truth in all things, walking the ONE path.
The mind, or as I prefer, awareness, plays a funny game.
It has the capacity to touch the stars, yet so often is just grounded in blind expectation.
The hardest thing for all of us perhaps, is the idea, well, the notion, of death for example.
As a moment for letting go of all the emotion we are aware of in the present.
From a sense of loss and sadness perhaps?
I believe,
The greatest trick in life is Total Acceptance and Full Forgiveness.
To remember that all things in life are based on personal choice; even death.
In this way we can consider all in retrospect with gratitude and love.
As a part of our process of growth and learning.
As something that is common to us all regardless of anything else.
Of filling our awareness with experience as we expand the same.
Searching for understanding, for balance to BEcome more.
More than just the emotional response of the beast.
And so, all the obstacles to happiness begin to dissolve away to nothing.

To begin, to expand your sense of self, consider this…
The limiting notions of affiliation to ANY THING at ANY LEVEL!
First, to this shell of your BEing.
BE grateful for this gift of a body. Treat it well, with love and respect.
But begin to understand how it will bend to your loving will at a cellular level.
In this way, you will avoid dis-ease and experience the benefit of a positive life body experience avoiding many limitations.
Limiting notions are only based on fear as opposed to truth.
Consider this and grow.
Then we can consider our family.
The family of the beast is a mishmash of awareness, experience and repetition of cycles.
Each cycle of repetition is unique, and thereby expansive in its purpose.
Here we search for awareness of the cycles, the unloving errors that hold us all back.
And so, we seek for nothing more than perfection in our Faith, Belief and expectation of self. Based on an expanding awareness of truth as we grow in courage and unconditional love for self and all, for we are all ONE after all.
Perhaps next, we see the division within national boundaries, by virtue of regions, of sectors, states and counties. The scales of division seen is never ending and the ways in which division can be realised seem endless.
Division based on gender, complexion, hair colour, lead hand. Race, religion, working group, education level, language, height, deviations from the norm - itself based on what is generally considered as common, delivering a "Normal" from expectation.
Income level, bank balance, etcetera etcetera.
It just continues as the ego yearns to separate and grow more

than other selves. To embrace a notion of superiority. The blindness is obvious when balanced against truth.

I have experienced much that is both good and bad here in this awareness; positive and negative, truth and error.

Yet in all things I have neither sought, nor seek, any external understanding or forgiveness from another. Things are as they are.

For the truth, in the growth of expanded awareness and greater understanding, is of a purely personal nature and relies on nothing more than self.

Self-awareness, self-forgiveness and self-love.

All forgiving, understanding, total ease in awareness, based on faith, as Belief in truth which sets me free.

Intention and Expectation, as the single key to create what we see, both internally and externally.

There is only one way to make a particular vibration. Or a specific picture of harmonies that show a unique distribution of colours.

That sounds like one song. That describes one thing.

So much energy working together to deliver a moment that transcends a single awareness, but is an amalgam of ALL which is ONE.

Sensed through independent feeds of awareness.

Cycles of existence, change.

Unique moments becoming effectual through ONE.

~*~

The biggest secret then, is that ALL the POWER that could ever BE required for any one and/or every other thing, was, is, and only ever will BE, based on the single awareness of self.

~*~

That place in which you seem to BE from.
That place which simply is YOU.
There is no limit then, to the imagination.
As the perceptions of our reality change, so reality is created, as a reflection of the desire expressed by someone. As an expression of the energy they used to create the way things are.
In this way, nothing is beyond manifestation.

.
...
......
....

"abracadabra"

Limitation

The "notion" of Limitation.
What level of... something, is the limit?
Within the notion of creation, why do some people see any limitation?
What could cause such a limitation?
Limits only exist in YOUR OWN awareness.
What IS the limit of 'your own' creativity?
Because creation is infinite it follows that all things are infinite in potential.
The nature of a specific existence taken further and further ad infinitum.
At what point in creative progression/expression do 'all things' become the same? When all retruns to source as source, as desired by source.
Is there a point at which all created becomes the same? Perhaps the beginning and the end?
First, we take a single point in awareness which also happens to be in this Universe (our current awareness).
We can consider this point as infinitesimally small.
We then have the smallest movement from point A (the point of origin), to a new, second point, point B. The distances are as short as is possible in awareness. So, that would be infinitesimally small.
Here we must consider the creation of the second point.

So, in our awareness we focus on a single point. Then another point. Then we think of something at point A firing off to engage in motion.
The notion of motion, as something is now "moving" "through SPACE"!
Space which was created in our own awareness. If it wasn't, it wouldn't BE there.
If we have a notion of movement we have created a thing which moved by virtue of space existing.

One could consider the notion of something moving from point A to point B; moving back and forth between these two points perhaps?
So, what if we just take a single point, A.
We fire off accordingly to produced energy. Energy is focussed on the point where it becomes infinite through achieving infinite frequency.
How is that possible? Because the blip of energy that increases is actually increasing from the same point of origin, one after the other until all potential directions have been achieved. This omni-directional flurry is a single point. A single light?
As the focus increases, the speed of the 'pulses' or 'firings', for want of better phrases, increases until it gets to the moment of achieving infinite speed, when it can no longer be contained within time/space and breaks out into space/time perhaps?

Here we are again; stuck in the notion of dimension!
(Remember that all notions born of here are just that, born of here. From this perspective. So, potentially limited?).
Can we consider movement from a point of origin, firing off as it were, omni-directionally? Creating a ball of light for the purpose of picturing this creation.
For within the darkness there came light.
We can consider this light element as one infinitesimally small. Of no fixed position (home), it simply exists in awareness.
All things get to a point of change.
All as described at the beginning of the book.
Space/time is created to support the existence of other in all that is, and so creation takes place.
It is worth noting here, that space/time comes from time/space.

Everything viewed from the other side is back to front perhaps. Think on that maybe?
A wideo on the difference between time/space and space/time can be found here;
https://youtu.be/Y8BbbSOTZPE (on the Roy Dow channel).
If we created from the beginning again here, would it manifest in a new space/time or be created as new in this space/time, all within the original time/space?
To break free of this space/time and enter the dimension of the omniverse, that of Time/Space, where movement is based on nothing more than awareness without reference to dimension or time, is to pierce the Veil/Law of confusion and peek at our true nature. What we actually are!
A dimensional awareness where position and moment (suggesting a reference to time, linear scale and spatial awareness), are of no consequence and therefore not considered.
An awareness of the many verses, of vibrational creation, can be found.
One must say infinite verses of course, as in the number of verses to which you, in awareness, become aware.

Could we conceive of a thing outside or beyond the awareness of the big g? No. Because our awareness IS that of the big g by way of expression as other self, a notion magnified by the use of the Veil/Law of Confusion.

Here then, we have found the realm of manifestation. Where all things are created within the confines of awareness. For awareness is all there is.
To create, one simply begins to create, in awareness.
Unlike the big g and the notions of a first creation, when after awareness, self-awareness, focus of the awareness, etcetera, and the creation of energy, the first movement even, we have the creation of the Universe (Time/Space Space/Time), to

accommodate the first movement given birth to!
Through the exploration of infinite vibrations (sound/light etcetera), all, in the literal sense, is created.
Once all the building blocks have been created, then the changes in unity can begin.
The infinite combinations of energy in growth, as in quantity and also in interactions with other creations, can begin to be explored.

The awareness of the creator then, is in a state of constant expansion as we (the creator expressed in an individual awareness of freewill), experience yet more input from all sources of creation.
Our own experiences (as perceived in our singular awareness), is born of freewill to maximise the potential for infinite combinations of the same. It also serves to hasten, with increased yearning and desire, the extension of negative polarisations which serve to balance with the extending of positive polarisations.
Balance is everything in creation. Hence the cessation of negative polarization as it becomes aware of wisdom. For in the balance of wisdom, we understand the nature of all, detached from notions of difference.
It is this very balance which serves as the optimum pathway in awareness. Awareness of the importance of balance leads to swift growth.
For through this awareness we can find the truth in creation. Which lends itself to our own understanding of the merits of following a path of balance, the 'Middle Way' as it were.
Unaffected by the pull of one or the other, in any sense.
Notions of good and bad, of morals and ethics, of ownership and theft. Of rights to this or that?
All of course, are of no consequence.
They are unimportant in the grand scheme of things. BUT,

everything is also important in the GRAND SCHEME of THINGS!

Because it is the small things that make up the big thing.

From back to the beginning, right up to the infinite experience, which is the joining of our own expanded awareness with the infinite awareness of creation and source.

Here we find the infinite intelligence spoke of.

The knowing of all things, as at current infinite limitations (which is always out of date), and which knows no limits of course.

As everything is vibration/energy, we can begin to become aware of what are the good vibes and what are the bad vibes so to speak. What serves us on our chosen journey and what doesn't.

Or to look at it another way, if all is played out in infinite time/space space/time scenarios, then in your current awareness you can begin to appreciate the benefits of existence in a world of balance!

For it is in the extremes that outcomes begin to evolve into over polarisation; leaning one way or the other! Good or bad?

Now we must translate the notion of balance in all things, addressed by the human BEan.

With a view to the best possible outcome from a balanced perspective in every aspect of existence, for every life awareness here and now!

Achieving this equates to the Paradise, or Eden, that so many have sought.

Because through the achievement of balance in all things, all awareness is balanced at a level of simply knowing all.

Knowing in this way suggests that nothing is of much consequence, yet is, for all paths lead to the same place.

Neither happy nor sad. Up or down. Just balanced. Nice. Acceptable.

This is the perfect state.
To aspire to this state of awareness is to move towards your own nirvana.
Your own bliss.
As we achieve a level of balance in our minds/awareness, we begin to open up to endless expansion of awareness in what is Truth.
New possibilities grow and present to your awareness, as you begin to create with more focus, to gain more specific results in your creativity.
This is the nature of the game.
To create all you want to create, anywhere, in any way. To expand your awareness and experience, which contributes to the whole as a resource for continuations of the same.
Go Beans!

peace not war

peace not war
and much, much more
is what I'd like to see

to see the people happy
in any community

religious bars should now come down
for they've been up too long

and if a catholic priest says come
a muslim goes along

this is what I'd like to see
a land that's full of life and free

a land where bombs are in the past
a time when peace on earth will last

roy thomas dow. circa 1972
(age 11-12yrs)

Don't Panic! Take Care Beans!

Not a warning, just truth

By Roy Thomas
12102021

It's never been my intention to appear as a harbinger of doom, gloom and despair, I simply share my awareness, which is my truth.
I share with love in my heart.
If you dismiss the notion of other self beyond or the existence of the big g (my name for god), often associated with spirituality, then you are transfixed by earth form and effectively, asleep.

If you have faith or a hope that Jesus of the bible will return to save you, my first thought is why do you believe you need saving; from what or who?
All I can think of is yourself.
All was ever done in his name and would ever be done again, is to share truth. Like the first time.
Why would things be any different when there is only ONE path. ONE way and ONE truth? So,
Wake up; BE present, BE aware, and consider the following, if you wish …

If someone claimed to BE the returning awareness of that person, saying I am Him, listen to me. I am Jesus Christ, Deal with it!
Would you simply consider them courting authority by virtue of a notion of authority attributed to the historical figure, then simply bestow that same reverence by virtue of those simple claims.

Having been here once, would you return with the same strategy? Would you know the potential for instant conflict, and thereby the seeming futility of such an approach?
What would be more important, the messages of truth or the recognition felt in an other self?
That jesus was awareness in the human shell is as true for us

today as for all in history. As such, advanced awareness can influence at any time. Just as negative polarities can influence.
Truth is as believed to be until growth in new awareness is obtained.
We are all expressions of the awareness of the big g. We vibrate according to our awareness, which rises as we acquire truth.
Truth focuses and refines. It balances and elevates.
With greater understanding comes tolerance, for knowing where others walk having walked the same, we can see where other self may be on that walk.
This, is empathy.
Knowing is based on experience, remember! Expereince is shared in all as ONE.
You have time to change with sincerity! Read on, this may not be what you think.
To view the behaviour (the expression of awareness), of some human animals as disgraceful, like those that kill, injure, abuse, bully or control to name a few ACTIONS, seems accurate. ALL THE ABOVE and more, will lower your vibration if these are actions you do.

The lowering of your vibration
IS BY YOUR HAND ALONE!

AS SUCH, YOUR REAP THE REWARDS AND BENEFITS OF ALL YOU SOW BY CHOICE.

YOUR FREE WILL
DETERMINES YOUR FUTURE
Simple.

Also, BE aware that this experience is based on FREE WILL. Singularly based on a notion of the big g in the awareness of all that is!

And so, to deny it, FREEWILL, to imprison another human animal in any way, the participation in or awareness of torment, torture or confinement of other self, is a most egregious act. It does NOTHING but demonstrate your Beast nature.

You are a Human animal. Fixed in earth form.

Consider the rage of a savage BEast. Control is lost completely. Are you a BEast?

Torment and torture; how can we even begin to comprehend how LOW this is vibrationally?

UNDERSTAND?

The gift of FREEWILL, IS the basis for your own responsibility towards self, regarding your chosen actions in this awareness; AND

THIS WHOLE PLANET AND THE VEIL OF CONFUSION, THE NOTION OF THE WHAT, AND THE WHY REGARDING THE PLANET AND THE VEIL, COMES FROM EXPANDED AWARENESS.

IF YOU CAN BEGIN TO GRASP THAT, YOU ARE GROWING IN AWARENESS.

WHATEVER you have done in this experience, you should KNOW that this is what you came here to do in all probability, BUT(!), with a view to learning from the experience thereby expanding your awareness and bringing into question your behaviour so you may determine that alternate choices are now a preference if required. This is Growth!

If you don't learn during your "Life", you cycle in the same 'opportunity', over and over until you Die/pass/move on.

I will celebrate completion for you on your passing.

If you fail to learn and expand your awareness by the time you pass (raising your vibration), clearly demonstrated in ALL your behaviour (thought, word, action), whereby you KNOW you are more than you were, then at the completion of this MAJOR CYCLE you may begin another MAJOR

CYCLE in a completely different experience aware of even higher vibration.

Failing to become aware is the risk in coming back, by choice, to learn again in this density, regardless of intention or prior experience and higher vibrations.
Trapped in the loop so to speak.
Be Aware that when you pass having finished your learning, you may find yourself in a place of VERY LOW Vibrational energy/awareness.
The reality of experience on passing is no less than you find here.
How so?
Because awareness is awareness. You are awareness. This IS the immortal you as it were.
So, the learning continues and the errors (perceived as that which is not the ONE path), are balanced in experience.

> You cannot understand the impact of action unless…,
> YOU ARE THE RECIPIENT OF THAT ACTION
> [OH DEAR? – True]

YOU, WILL BE THE RECIPIENT OF THE VERY ACTION YOU CHOSE TO TAKE HERE IN YOUR AWARENESS INCLUDING THAT ACTION INSTIGATED, AS IT'S IN YOUR AWARENESS.
ALL TO BALANCE THE NATURE OF YOUR AWARENESS.

What goes around, comes around, in the fullness of… awareness, not time in this instance!
If the Jesus of the new testament had not repented in the final moments before passing, he too would have become lost on the Karmic Wheel due to his awareness of the death of a

slightly older youth in his own childhood, and the circumstances surrounding the same.

Because we are simply talking about vibrational rates as determined by your thoughts, words and actions; what you are vibrationally, determines where you find yourself on passing.

Know...

There is ONE path, and that which is not!

As the notion of other path is gone within another 3 densities, it becomes plain that the deceptions of many (and upon many), engaged in pursuits that take you away from the ONE Path, are just that. Deceptions.

Immersed in the yellow rays of intelligence, you might attempt to rationalise the following, all you atheists? Or those that self-serve with a view towards that which is not.

So, the big g (who is beyond the universe), who created the universe within self, with a view to experience other self, will develop (within self), a rebellion.

Multiple personality disorder perhaps?

How do YOU in awareness, begin to QUANTIFY the nature of the big g with a view to overcoming/dominating the creator of ALL that is? Clearly a nonsense then.

Normally we could consider a deluded self, but watching the first video on "God, the universe & us + the god particle and the principle of consciousness", suggests otherwise.

Let us consider Repentance.

Repentance = expanding awareness.

Listen, Think. See, Grow, create with Love

A full awareness of error and a sincere desire to stop the action of error of self, to BE MORE than you were.

(NB),

Without repentance, you display ignorance towards error and

so remain unenlightened as to the grace/awareness available in these instances for your own growth.
To expanded beyond that which was current for you. Those lower vibrations you have risen beyond to become aware of below you so to speak.
"I will rise above…"
Be aware to the demented behaviour of the lower human animal awareness/ego.
Be present and pause, question all you think, say and do.
Increase the grace of god in your awareness.
There but for the grace of god go I. So, move away from the energy when grace is found.
Grace then is truth, truth in your own awareness.
Seek the comfort of the higher mind. The higher awareness.
Walk the ONE path.
As the pen is mightier than the sword, maybe we ought to consider meaning?

Repent.
feel or express sincere regret or remorse about one's wrongdoing or sin:
Do not entertain guilt for there is no sin. Just KNOW, what is the action of a seeker on the ONE path and what IS NOT!
"I am aware of what I did, and I sincerely wish I hadn't done it. I regret my actions. I now have new awareness and I won't do it again".
This is the greatest achievement here! This is personal progress. This is your job. To expand your awareness in truth as the pursuit of knowing the ONE creator.
BELIEF/Awareness/pertaining to truth?
ORIGIN mid 16th century (originally in the senses 'belief', 'credibility'): from French crédit, probably via Italian credito from Latin creditum, neuter past participle of credere 'believe, trust'.

SPIRITUALITY
the quality of being concerned with the human spirit or soul as opposed to material or physical things.
DEMENTED
behaving irrationally due to anger, distress, or excitement: she was demented with worry. From Old French dementer or late Latin dementare, from demons 'out of one's mind'.

With NEW in your awareness, or old awareness rekindled, either makes no difference, know your thoughts, words and actions makes a difference.
That's all.

Change begins now, if you wish

By Roy Thomas Dow
31102021

Say it loud and say it clear, to understand and say it here
When I read or watch or listen, as I sit, upon the orb
Truly, do I grow in love, co-creating, to absorb.

Feel it, think it, BE it - true, see awareness shared with you
Words in rhyme to entertain, spoken riddle, all is plain
Nonsense then, recline relax, seeking self on soulful tracks...

~*~

Hello Beans

I feel compelled to share, and so I do, to the extent that I am, and nothing more, for it is all I can to BE.
Energy, is in motion. I am experiencing e motion.
Words always bring change, because they produce energy in motion in others, as well as yourself.
A responsibility then!
Comfort doesn't always have to BE happy. Comfort can be found in the darkest place.
This is where people often feel deep disturbances in truth; realisations and moments of re-energising old scars and pains from other awareness.

Other awareness can anchor us in a specific cycle. All cycles can BE stopped; as simply as "Now, I stop, and look, and listen".
So, that's what you do. Simple.
To see the cycle is to BE, beside it. To BE detached in an awareness, but an awareness nonetheless; this is presence.
Presence allows me to view with different eyes.
In all other self I see creator, I see divine in potential. I see hope, love, tenderness compassion, empathy. Frustrations,

fears, anger, envy greed lusts.
I see no good, I see no evil.
I see opportunity for knowing and expressing self, based on desire and on self-control. Expressed through free will.
To me, there is simply awareness, and choices made in moments based on what a self or other self (me, everyone else), determines.
Sometimes you realise, you can't change people so 'forget 'em'. The F E principle.
Sometimes you realise you can't change a situation, 'a now' or 'a history' perhaps, so 'forget it'. The F I principle.
The f an' f's have stood me in good stead for years. It stops you wasting your own e motion (energy in motion), on them and yourself, based on un-desirable energies BEing felt in your awareness.
If these feelings are in your awareness, they stay there by your choice. So are also removed from your awareness if you feel they no longer serve YOU. Another choice. If the world forgave itself might we find peace?
And awareness continues. Growth in awareness continues; You continue.

Action has the responsibility for self within it, and nothing more. It displays nature as choice.
The only questions you need to answer, are these.
Are You, aware of how the BEast manifests in You? So many different ways of course!
Knowing this, is the first step in controlling your BEast energies as it were. Controlling the not so nice you, that sits in full potential, in all of us. Know this, so you can lose all judgement.This is how we raise our vibration and change our behaviour for good. For the good of self and the good of other self. As you expand your awareness, you raise your vibration, refining your energy.

Controlling yourself, you project higher vibes. Attracting other higher vibes, and enhancing the vibes of all those who come into contact with you.

Not by BEing weird and freaking people out, but by your example of self-control, of balance and personal growth.

Embracing the power in free will for self, and thereby acknowledging the need for the same for all Beans, now!

In that you are aware of self or other self, and the dualities for reference by the energy we choose to use. That of the nature of BEast? Or do we choose to elevate self, using free will? Knowing the answer to that question, as we always do, sets our fate as it were! We simply choose an action, based on desire. We sow we reap.

Know your thoughts, words and deeds therefore. As seeds of deeds beyond current awareness, grow! Know this.

To accept other self as well as self, due to this truth can BE relieving in itself. Begin to make different choices, NOW!

As I consider the actions of others in my life, I find I forgive them; understanding, seeing the plan, the learning, the truth to set me free.

I gain the power of control over the awareness and so now choose(!) to release the cycles I no longer need. I have grown, and keep on growing. Growing in the truth that is MY growing awareness. The same as YOUR growing awareness is yours.

I see the weakness in other's thoughts, words and actions as the cycles of emotional catalyst repeat and repeat beating the life out of them, and those they choose to engage with much and more of the same. *I hold onto the truth in awareness of choice BEing that of the individual, always.*

Always by choice it seems! Individual choice. Take control of you! BE free!

To truly see it, is to sometimes feel alone ("can't you see this"? - you may think to yourself). Silence is Golden isn't it? A comfort? Not always.

Beginning to grasps the notion of your own immortality and purpose. To expand your awareness. To know and feel the limitless nature of creation that is here for YOU. For all of US.

Knowing can lead to frustrations, which is a part of that learning. Seeking Wisdom.

Love yourself, embracing the experience of truth in knowing who you are, why you're here, and how you 'Will' BE. by choice, by your own hand, in control of self, BE cause you are, BE cause you can, BE cause YOU, WILL IT SO and nothing else!

If our actions define us to the world, and our words prepare them, WE must BE our thoughts, as it's that awareness which we are and all that's left, beyond.

For from this infinite place of knowing all our essence in BEing is derived... if, we pause to BE aware!
Which, is to Tame the BEast, within self.
See the WAY of THE BEast, and YOU begin to understand the NATURE of the BEast; and at that moment you ARE differentiating SELF FROM BEast.
Here, is seen the truth then; think on that!
The truth in you, your nature your BEing, your infinite potential, your magnificence, the wonder of it all. The great simplicity that is... Knowing.

And so, the first cycle in awakening is experienced.
It comes to completion as the possibility/probability of understanding and so knowing, immortality in self, ergo in all other

self, and so the realisation of creator in all of us becomes apparent... Aware then, of the potential of ONE.

The notion of infinite potential and process accepted because we just know now. So, we relax... WE Breath, and take it all in.
Fear melts away in our minds, and the truth in our own existence is a new awareness.
Of a different idea; new desires perhaps?
More carefree, more acceptance of other self, just BEing.

The notion of clear thoughts, based on love and truth. Loving self, BE cause, we can.
Because, it is a celebration of simply knowing. Feeling reassured, with our faith, based on SEEING.
The truth has set us Free

All Aboard!

That I could dream a hundred lives and never once feel free
And BE the king in every one, yet never could see thee
To never know if all was good or all was right as it should be
Yet always finding peace and bliss when resting up against a tree

To never truly feel that cross that I could ever see such pain
No anger, really? Never loss, for truly all we see is gain
There's truth in every grain in nature, wonder in each drop of rain
Spinal taps release the seed, that seeks to rest within the brain

Onward ever onward up and down again we seem to go
Time in never ending cycles, leading to the ONE you know
Always, is there love for you that you create so you can show
The you, Yourself, that's deep inside, that always you find love to grow

Then as you grow, you surely see, the light that's deep inside of thee
The love, a fire, in your soul, that you may dig like morris mole
Deep within without a care, you do it all BEcause you dare
And yes, you dare BEcause you know, there's only ONE, and so you grow

This is the way it always IS, the way was always meant to BE
A path to ONE or not at all, a simple choice for you and me
A final call, a chance encounter? Always, god will find a way
Rest assured, that once you've slept, your sight will greet another day.

Begin to choose, and set intent, to sow the seeds of all you are
That you can start to build a home, again to wish upon a star
Then as the seed begins to grow, some truth is in awareness found
Reaching high towards the sun, strong foundations in the ground

Silence in the voice eternal, calm and quiet is the way
Knowing all is for the seeker, knowing it most every day
Every day the seeker grows and understands a little more
Hidden secrets, such a nonsense, ONE, is just an open door

So, choose! For time is running out, the grains of sand they disappear
You know the song the choice the word, you see it all, I made it clear
You cannot say you didn't know, you can't say you don't understand
The only thing you need to know, your future lies within your hand.

By Roy Thomas
07102021

My Anytime (daily) prayer.

~*~

I am Whole, Perfect, Strong.

Powerful, Loving, Harmonious and Happy.

I Am the Universe, I am all there is.

For the light of my Father is all that there is,

And I AM that Light.

I and my Father are ONE.

~*~

So be it – The big g

I pray for myself, and all beans,
that we may ever grow in love/light light/love;

and ultimately
change ourselves, and our world.

The changes are here, now.
For all of us

Mind your thoughts
Mind your words
Mind your actions

Pray to the big g

Go with god

please visit these sites,
if necessary, keep returning

return until something is there.

then you'll know what to do

roydow.com
changetheworldnow.org

(coming soon?)
mycff.org
communityfoodfunding.com
+

Other titles avalable at 1331PRESS

Strawberry Angel and the Bean
a love story as old as time.

This epic ryming poem (just shy of 40,000 words), transports you to the world of faires, goblins, witch, and warlock. Forest creatures, daring deeds! Of *hooman* BEans, searching for growth through the Alchemy of change...

(extract)

5

From out the darkness of a dream, a place of still and wonder true
   Did first I catch a glimpse of thee, and thee of I, to see was new
      That knowing deep inside, once felt, can never send away
   A love that sparked so true and pure, then captured me that day

   Strawberry angel, darling fairy, tell me that it's true
   Speak it true thy love for me, as though you always knew
 'Tis now mine eyes did find you, like you came from far away
   And instantly lock onto to you, to dream you every day

~*~

"Remember, the WORD we hear, is enough to change our BEing."

Roy Thomas. 20122021

Echoes from the Soul
the first Anthology

"Poetry, is always, a heartfelt expression."
Roy T~~~~~mas.

If you e~~~~ ~~~~~ verse, with strong tempo, giving clear messages to move ~~~~
Then here you will n~~ ~~~~~~~ ~bstance, meaning and passion, fun and frivolity.
If you seek to journey in rhyme, t~ ~~~~~~ ~ract, to grasp the subtleties of personal awareness shared~
Look no further.   This book *is* for you!

WITHDRAWN - To be retitled

~*~

"creating and sharing my poetry is perhaps a core purpose?
A passion for which I am grateful"

"This anthology combines poems from when I was much younger, to whispers from age and ex-perience. The desire to write poetry has been strong over the past few years, and there is a strong spiritual bias in most poems; something that reflects my own journey, here and now.
The need to share strong and unshakable spiritual impressions at this time, is something I do with pleasure; in the hope it will expand a notion within, for yourself; the messages being short and clear."

~*~

Audio Books from 1331PRESS

This is the most up to date list of Audio books planned for release in the first during 2022.
They are not in any specific order.

Strawberry Angel and the Bean.
The epic adventure of love and resurrection.

Echoes of the Soul (Title Withdrawn - to be retitled).
The first anthology, has a strong spiritual bias to assist where possible shifts in awareness, found in truths shared!

Expanding Awareness
The guide for altering your awareness with expanded truths, covering the beginning, creation, the universe and of course us, our purpose and future.

~*~

All published works are released as ebooks, Print on Demand paperbacks and Audio books (where possible).
Different formats may be released on different dates.

For more up to date release date details, see the 1331PRESS page, on
roydow.com or at changetheworldnow.org.

Publishers note to the Reader.

The Author welcomes all feedback.
Please write in the first instance to;

>"Author"
>c/o 1331PRESS
>PO Box 228
>Wondai. Qld. 4606. Australia

www.ingramcontent.com/pod-product-compliance
Lightning Source LLC
Chambersburg PA
CBHW071617080526
44588CB00010B/1161